TRAVEL WRITING 101

Everything You Need To Know To Start The Best Job In The World

30+ 'how to' lessons from professional travel writers and editors

TravelWriteEarn.com

D1506286

CONTENTS

'Voice'

EDITORS
James Durston, Kim Lambert, Ffion Llwyd-Jones, David Mumpower, Rachael Rowe

CONTRIBUTORS
Niche Writing And Finding Ideas
Judith Fein, Elyse Hauser, Kristine Jepsen, Scott Kendall, Katherine Martinelli, Qin Xie

How To Write With Meaning, Impact and Personality
Sandra Henriques, Kim Lambert, Wayne Moran, Diana Plater, Rachael Rowe

Fees, Finances And The Business Of Writing
Christa Bedwin, Lucy Bryson, MaryRose Denton, Andrew Madigan

Relationships And Client Management
Lindy Alexander, Chez Chesak, David Mumpower, Jo Ostgarden

Pitching, Credentials And The Sell
John Malathronas, PJ Heller, Deborah Mackie

Blogging And Social Media
Shobha George, Betsi Hill, Ashley Howe, Fiona Maclean, Sue Reddel, Rossana Wyatt

SO YOU WANT TO BE A TRAVEL WRITER...

Introduction by James Durston

But what is a travel writer, exactly?"

The question came from a friend. We were sitting in a bar in Singapore, a plastic chairs and table affair, the evening's humidity condensing into rivers on our beer bottles. I stifled a smirk. This guy was a journalist, had a PhD in something to do with PR and the media, and he felt the need to ask a question like that? Was he taking the piss? I dabbed three tributaries of sweat from my neck, then paused. It's possible it was a good question. What's the difference between a travel writer and any other writer? What makes an article a travel article, specifically?

It's not easy to pick an answer. The travel publishing industry covers so many genres, article types, topics and themes, to try to define it precisely would be like trying to paint a rainbow with a single color. There are memoirs, travelogues, first-person narratives, third-person reviews, itineraries, photo-essays, listicles, op-eds, investigative features, guidebooks, and more. Subjects can include people, art, culture, restaurants, accomodation, technology, destinations in and of themselves, shopping experiences, tours, things that went badly, things that went well, things to do, see, taste, touch, smell and more, again.

Probably for this reason 'travel writing' is something most budding, or even experienced freelance writers try at least once or twice. Some make a living at it. Others do it part-time, when they can afford to. Still more fail, unwilling or unable to compete with so many other wannabe travel writers for every single paycheck. Don't be fooled - if you hear 'travel writer' and imagine a cocktail-sipping, journal-writing bohemian lounging on a Fijian beach one day, sauntering up Paris' Champs-Élysées another, occasionally filing pensive missives back to editorial HQ where editors gush lovingly over every purple paragraph, you're in for a shock. That can and does happen, but infrequently, and that kind of lifestyle dream is best reserved for retirees and others who have transcended the annoying chore of having to earn money each month.

Those who want to earn a regular income writing about their travels need to consider it a job, and not a very well paid one. But - here's the good news - there are many things you can do to give yourself an advantage over others, and this book goes into the details of nearly all of them.

This book is a cooperative project between more than 30 travel writers and editors, with a cumulative experience of many decades. There is no single way to become a travel writer. Even better, there's not just one way to earn money in the travel writing business. If you asked all the contributors here to describe the paths they took to travel writing success, I'm sure you would get 30 different answers. The old-fashioned, and often still most aspirational way to earn money as a travel writer is to sell your stories to magazines, newspapers and websites. This is what we can call 'travel journalism' - high quality ideas, expressed with high quality writing that earns a decent fee and is published by a third party. But the age of the internet and of blogging in particular has added many other methods, from affiliate marketing to sponsored posts to saleable social media chats and more. If all that seems rather overwhelming, don't worry, you're not alone. Consider this book a friendly cohort of 30 people who were once in your position, and are now here by your side urging you on with advice and inspiration. And a good bit of perspiration too.

You don't need qualifications to be a freelance writer, but you do need knowledge, and the more you have before you start out on what could become an adventurous, glamorous and perhaps even lifelong career, the better your chances of hitting that road running.

So what makes a travel writer? I'll tell you what I told my friend in Singapore, as he eyed me suspiciously. "A travel writer is someone who travels, then writes, so they can travel some more, so they can write some more, so they can travel more ..."

Good luck.

JD

NICHE WRITING AND FINDING IDEAS

FOREWORD BY DAVID MUMPOWER

How much do you care about steampunk cosplay or canine fashion wear or cryptocurrency arbitrage? Your answer is probably none, but somebody clearly cares about each one. They all have millions of Google search results.

Now, let's think about the situation in a different way. How many people do you believe are experts in the field of cryptocurrency arbitrage? Could any of your friends write an engaging story about the best choices in canine fashionwear? How would you compile a piece on the future of steampunk cosplay?

What Are My Interests And Passions?

The reality is that humanity doesn't have One True Topic that everyone enjoys. Instead, the nature of conversation dictates that all eight billion of us have individual interests. And someone needs to fill the void in expressing thoughts on each one. As a freelance writer, that's where the money is.

Let's be honest. You'll discover intense competition when you try to publish a book or lock down a recurring gig writing about celebrity gossip. Many would-be content creators share those interests. Writing about something that's outside of a person's comfort zone is what distinguishes the professionals from the wannabes.

Someone somewhere wants a respectful article about canine fashionwear. Even when you agree with Monica Geller that "animals dressed as humans" is one of your biggest pet peeves, you still can't be dismissive about such potential articles. You must approach any story in an engaging manner that will impress readers and earn you more work.

Here's the dirty little secret of freelance writing today. Any article that has your name on it works as a resume, a demonstration of your skill or *gulp* lack thereof. You need to find work whenever and wherever you can to build the strength of that resume. Sadly, some of the assignments you get will fall into these niche categories outside your area of expertise, even within the travel industry. So, what do you do?

Everyone You Meet Has A Potential Story

For starters, let this section be your guide. We have six experts in the field of freelance travel writing, and they've all boldly gone off the beaten path with their career trajectories, as any self-respecting traveler should.

Some are expatriates who have developed viable monetization strategies through their multi-cultural experiences. Others are world travelers who mitigate the cost of their vacations by writing stories about their travels. One is even a college professor who educates young minds on the art of the pitch.

These freelance writers will provide you with their life lessons and professional experiences. They'll pass along proven tactics for successful article pitches. These suggestions could make you a lot of money.

A couple of the contributors in this section have also worked on the other side. They've spent years accepting pitches from others. They know the best approaches and also relay several examples of what not to do.

One contributor shares his personal history. He

details how his love for his son has empowered him to improve his writing and pay for his European travels. Anyone who wants to work as a freelancer to pay for travel should heed his advice.

Shop Where The Locals Shop

Similarly, a mother explains how her children's interactions have guided her to several innovative story ideas. She encapsulates a different kind of niche pitch, one created out of necessity. After all, in any community, kids share many of the same social and physical needs. Alert parents will realize just how many pitches have been right under their noses at every childrens' gathering.

Also in this section, an award-winning author details her secret weapon, a technique certain to give freelancers better ideas for pitches. She shares personal experiences in foreign cultures wherein her natural intellectual curiosity has produced professional dividends. This tactic is sure to help you expand the range of your pitches.

Similarly, a veteran writer/editor demonstrates several tricks of the trade. She examines the importance of story angles, preferably novel approaches. And she highlights publications that freelancers may find receptive to such nuanced pitches. She'll even explain how to become a successful travel writer without going any-where.

Lay The Groundwork Once And Reap the Bene-fits Multiple Times

Serendipitously, another chapter delves deeper into the same thought process. A master of the pitch explains how to turn one story idea into several potentially lucrative articles. She details how a single pitch possesses value with numer-ous different outlets.

Finally, this section ends with a brilliant piece about the current state and projectable future of freelancing. This eye-opening deconstruction of the profession will force you to re-evaluate your preconceived notions about your career aspir-ations. And it'll better prepare you for the real-ities of this vocation.

As a niche writer for 20 years and counting, I wish that I'd read all these pieces before I bun-gled into my career. It would have saved me any number of professional disappointments and unforced errors.

Take heed of all the wisdom contained in this section, and I'd advise you to compile notes while you read. There's tens of thousands of dol-lars of work suggested here...as long as you're willing to unearth the travel writer's equivalent to steampunk cosplay, canine fashionwear, and cryptocurrency arbitrage.

* * *

When David's not at Walt Disney World, he's writing about travel, movies and box office analysis, economics, streaming media, technology, and parks & recreation. He's the author of the Disney Demystified and Behind the Ride book series.

BECOME AN IDEA FACTORY: HOW TO SELL MULTIPLE STORIES FROM EVERY EXPERIENCE

How to expand your reach -- and your revenue -- by turning one article idea into many.

By Katherine Martinelli

T hese days, being a successful travel writer includes a lot of bootstrapping and creative thinking. If you've just been writing one story per topic you're covering, you're working harder than you have to and not earning as much as you could. And if you've only been focused on travel publications, then you are missing out on a world of potential markets.

Of course, after a trip, you might sell multiple stories about a particular destination, but getting in the habit of exploring multiple story angles for every topic is a helpful exercise for finding new story ideas and increasing revenue.

Here we'll talk about the dos and don'ts of selling multiple versions of the same premise to multiple publications, and we will walk through the brainstorming process. You'll be left with the tools to turn one seed of an idea into many, thus increasing your reach.

Finding Multiple Story Ideas from One Premise

A good travel article takes a lot of work. You have to get to the destination, get to know it, talk with local experts if you aren't one yourself, and come up with story ideas. Then, of course, you'll pitch, sell, and write the articles. But if you can come up with multiple angles, you can lay the groundwork once and reap the benefits multiple times.

One of the easiest ways to do this is to think beyond straight travel publications. Sure, you can start there for your big, main ideas. But once you have that seed, then start to think about other niches like food, business, science and the environment, real estate, pop culture, parenting, politics, and history. By using some creative thought and expanding your reach, one story idea can become many.

Let's look at how this might look in practice. We'll take a very broad starting point: The Statue of Liberty. Is there anything new to write about an iconic landmark like the Statue of Liberty? It would seem not, and yet as long as people are lining up to visit, there will be room for new stories about it.

Here are a few ways you can come up with fresh ideas while expanding your scope. To show you how this process works, here are some possible story angles for different publications with a hed (headline) and dek (subheading) for each:

Travel
Hed: Everything you need to know about visiting the Statue of Liberty
Dek: With strict rules about what you can bring and how to get up to the crown, you need to plan ahead.

Hed: Top hacks for managing a visit to the Statue of Liberty during peak season
Dek: Millions of people visit Lady Liberty every year, most in the summer. Here's how to beat the lines—and the heat.

Hed: 5 ways to get a great—and free—view of the Statue of Liberty
Dek: It's not a trip to NYC without seeing Lady Liberty, but there are ways to do it without the hassle of an official tour.

Food
Hed: 5 restaurants that have a great view of the Statue of Liberty
Dek: For the ultimate iconic New York experience, grab a table at one of these eateries with a view.

Hed: Where to grab a bite after a visit to the Statue of Liberty
Dek: What used to be a culinary dead zone is now a foodie destination.

Business
Hed: The Statue of Liberty brings in $263.2 million in revenue each year—where does it go?
Dek: Running a national landmark takes a lot of dough, but not without benefits.

Hed: How American Express saved the Statue of Liberty while increasing their own revenue
Dek: A look back at the revolutionary campaign

that sparked a trend in cause-related marketing.

Environment

Hed: The Statue of Liberty is one of the country's most popular tourist attractions. But at what cost to the environment?

Dek: A look at what happens when millions of tourists descend on the tip of Manhattan each year.

Hed: The world's only park ranger based in a city

Dek: Think all park rangers are stationed in the deep woods? Meet one who looks over the Statue of Liberty.

See how one basic premise can become a jumping off point for dozens of story ideas? These are just a few very loose ideas so you can get the basic idea of how this might work in practice.

Other ways to inspire ideas: keep an eye on anniversaries (there will be lots of coverage about the Statue of Liberty for its 150th anniversary, for example, but you could even pitch something for its 145th anniversary that is coming up); national holidays (Independence Day is an obvious tie-in here); and themed months (like Women's History Month).

Another approach is to think about various round-ups that you can build around one specific place or idea. You can zoom out (a listicle of the most popular tourist destinations in the country, or the world) or zoom in (a round-up of top sites in the city, popular sites that are worth the long lines (or not!)), landmarks that were gifts from other countries, places to eat or hotels to stay in near a certain landmark, etc.

Things not to do

Now that you've got the gist of how to spin one story in many ways, it's also important to cover what not to do. When done improperly, this tactic could get you blacklisted from publications. So here are some things to keep in mind:

As a general rule, **it's important not to sell the same story idea to two publications**. Even if they are in different genres doesn't mean you can write a slightly different version of the same story twice. While different angles, as discussed above, are usually fine, something like profiling the same person for two publications within a short time span is a no go. This can be tricky territory, so if ever in doubt: check your contract and/or ask your editor. Some publications have specific rules about waiting a certain amount of time (six weeks or six months) before publishing a story with a competitor on the same topic.

Never plagiarize, even from yourself. When you sell a story, you are selling original work (unless it's a reprint, see the next point), and editors do not look favorably on getting material that has clearly been recycled. So, find another way to describe Lady Liberty.

Don't resell a published article to another publication without permission. Just because you wrote it doesn't necessarily mean you own the rights. Check your contract, or negotiate to get the rights after a certain period of time. On the other end, be transparent that this article was first published elsewhere. Seek out publications that accept reprints. When done thoughtfully, this can be another way to get more dollars—or at least exposure—out of a single article.

Be careful when selling different angles to competitors. Publications can be fussy about seeing a similar story covered by the same person in a publication they perceive to be a competitor, which is why looking to different markets is a great tactic. It means the angle—and the audience—should be different enough that it won't be a problem. Again, when in doubt, check in with your editor. If you are on good terms with them and are transparent, then you'll avoid problems. At the end of the day, it's less about legal ramifications (though that can certainly come into play depending on how egregious the situation is) and more about journalistic ethics and maintaining a good reputation.

If you are interviewing one source for multiple stories, be very upfront about that—both to the source and the publications. Most will be totally cool with it, but some may not, and it's important to let those involved decide. Also, this should go without saying, but don't re-use quotes across multiple stories.

Your turn

Now it's your turn! To practice this idea, take one place you've visited, one restaurant where you've eaten, one person you've talked to, and write them down. Then, try to come at it from multiple angles. At first, it might just be a question like when was it built? How many visitors are there each year? What has happened to real estate values here over the years? When is peak season? And so on.

Try to go through at least a few of the topics you might be interested in and see how many story angles you can spin. Once you start, it's actually pretty fun. If it's helpful, you can use a chart like this to fill in your ideas:

Story idea seed:

	Story 1	Story 2	Story 3
Travel			
Food & Drink			
Pop Culture			
Science/Environment			
Parenting			
Business			
Real Estate			

Politics/History			

* * *

Katherine Martinelli is an award-winning journalist who has written for publications like The New York Times, Travel + Leisure, AFAR, Fodor's, Food & Wine, Smithsonian, The Atlantic, and many others. A native New Yorker who spent four years living in Israel, Katherine now calls Michigan home, where she lives with her husband and two kids.

HOW TO FIND YOUR OWN TRAVEL WRITING NICHE

A jack of all trades is a master of none. As a travel writer, pick your niche and become the recognized master of your domain.

By Scott Kendall

Most travel writers find themselves writing within one or more travel niches, rather than writing about anything and everything. The selected niche is usually centered around a writer's personal experiences and interests, or maybe by circumstances.

For example, my main niches are European Travel, Golf, Wineries, Breweries, and Distilleries, and Restaurants. This doesn't mean I only write stories that fit these niches, but I will normally focus on one or more of these topics.

Addressing a specific niche or niches makes sense. Everyone is familiar with, comfortable with, and knowledgeable about certain subjects. A writer may have special accessibility to certain people and places that others don't. And certain life circumstances may place the writer in the right place at the right time to cover a particular niche.

Advantages and Disadvantages

There are advantages and disadvantages of writing for a specific niche. Here are a few:

Advantages
Less competition – fewer people will be writing about your niche
Clarity of focus on specific destinations, subjects, and outlets
Fun and satisfaction of learning more about your area of interest
Opportunity to focus energy and time on a particular subject and become a subject expert
Once established as a subject expert, editors and clients will come to you

Disadvantages

Fewer outlets to choose from
Fewer sources for getting information on a limited subject
Sometimes more long-distance planning and preparation are required
Fewer contacts and networking channels

So, how did I choose European Travel as one of my major niches? Understanding the process I went through may help you choose the niche that fits you best.

When deciding what niche to write for, I asked myself a few questions. Here are some of those questions with my responses below. You can ask yourself the same questions to help determine your own niches.

What are my interests and passions?
What am I familiar with?
What opportunities do I have?
What editors and publications can serve as an outlet for my writing?

Interests

I am infatuated with learning more about other places, whether domestic or overseas. I especially love Europe for its history, architecture, natural wonders, interesting people, and more. Not only do I love the travel itself, but I also truly enjoy the research, the planning, making connections with people, and figuring out the logistics of my trips.

I have a passion for digging deeper and learning more about the places I visit. I happily talk to people, take pictures and videos, make notes, and truly try to understand the local cultures. And, most importantly for a travel writer, I get great satisfaction creating a story that ties all the facts, the stories, the personalities, the photos, and the history together into an enjoyable read.

I just returned from 16 days in southern England – London/Bath/Cotswolds -- and northern and central France – Paris/Loire Valley/Mont Saint Michel/Normandy/Giverny. In preparation for this trip, for over half a year, I researched my destinations, made plans, did more research, and revised plans some more. But these tasks weren't drudgery or chores. I genuinely enjoyed it, because I have an insatiable curiosity and deep-rooted interests in learning more about my destinations.

What are your interests? What fascinates you? If you have free time, or are planning trips for you and/or your family, what do you focus on? What would you like to learn more about? Remember, your niche is your niche, and you can create one out of whatever interests grab you.

Familiarity

Before I began travel writing, I had been to Europe a total of four times – twice to Germany and once each to England and Italy. Not a ton of experience, but enough to know that I wanted to go back and see more. I have also read lots of novels, seen movies, and studied up on European history, and I have always been fascinated by that part of the world.

Think about what you are familiar with. Where have you been? What have you read about, researched, talked about, and dreamed about? Think about where your previous travels have taken you as well as your experiences with your job, your hobbies, and your interests.

Opportunity

Being a school teacher and tennis coach and having my summers off is a huge advantage. I also get a week at Thanksgiving, two weeks at Christmas, and a week at Spring Break. I could go to Europe for two or three weeks during the summer and still have over a month off to write, travel more, and do other things.

For the last four summers, I have taken trips to Europe for two to three weeks at a time, and I don't plan to stop. For many other professions, it would be tough to take that much time off each year for travel. On a side note, I will be retiring from teaching and coaching soon and will have even more time to plan, travel, and write.

Another unique opportunity for me to write about Europe arose when my son, a captain in the Air Force, got orders to deploy to Aviano, Italy. I already had an interest in Europe, and now I had another powerful motivator to travel there – to see my son. So, for three summers in a row, I was able to travel to Italy to see Europe as well as to spend time with my son.

Your opportunities will be unique to you. What are your current and previous jobs? What contacts have you made, personally and professionally, that may give you an inside track? Consider who you know, where they are, and what contacts they may have that could help you. Do you travel on your job? You may be surprised at the opportunities you have because of your current situation and past experiences.

Relationships with Editors

As every writer knows, without an outlet to publish our stories, we are just writing for an audience of one – ourselves. And perhaps our partners or close friends. Luckily, early in my career, I queried the editor of a European publication for a story on a wonderful agriturismo (farm-stay) near San Gimignano I visited the summer before when I was planning a return. She commissioned the piece and since that first article I have written over a dozen articles covering my trips to Italy, Germany, Slovenia, Croatia, England, and France for this same editor.

I always do my best to communicate clearly with her. I also try to write interesting, useful articles with top quality photos and meet all deadlines. Before I send her my stories, I proofread and edit several times and clearly indicate where each carefully selected photo goes within the text. I want to make her job as editor as easy as possible, so she doesn't have to struggle with editing and understanding my submissions.

Make a list of editors you have worked with, or would like to work with. Make contact on TravMedia and LinkedIn. Send emails introducing yourself. Go to networking events, travel shows, and other places where editors, writers, and PR folks hang out. Send well written queries to those editors you would like to write for. Remember, even if an editor doesn't say yes to that particular query, a well written query can pique their interest and pave the way for possible future opportunities.

A Well-Chosen Niche Can Lead to Success

Choosing travel in Europe as one of my main niches has resulted in great success for me. I've had countless experiences throughout exciting parts of Europe.

In Slovenia, I ziplined and went white water rafting through gorges and rivers in the beautiful Soca River Valley, dined in fairytale Castle Bled overlooking the gorgeous Lake Bled, and toured the fabulous city of Ljubljana with its dragons and famous Triple Bridge.

In Giverny, I crossed the Japanese Bridge, strolled through the gardens, gazed at the water lilies and wandered through the art studio where Monet completed some of his most famous paintings.

In Paris, I came face to face with Mona Lisa in The Louvre, walked hand-in-hand along the Seine River with my honey as the Eiffel Tower twinkled high above and sampled wine in an ancient cellar established by King Louis XV's sommelier.

In Bath, I felt the heat of the steaming spring waters in the ancient Roman Baths, listened to the children's choir sing in the magical Bath Abbey and had tea and scones with Mr. Darcy looking over my wife's shoulder, at Jane Austen's Tearoom.

In The Cotswolds, I slept in King Charles I's bed, ate a delicious Sunday roast beef dinner at the historic Howard Arms, and stared in wonder at Owlpen Manor, described by Forbes as possibly "the loveliest place in England."

I look forward to many more adventures in Europe. It's my niche and I can make it into whatever I want to. What's your niche?

Write on!

* * *

Scott Kendall is a travel writer based in The Woodlands, Texas. His published work can be seen at scottkendalltravels.com.

LIVE LIKE A LOCAL, AND STORIES THAT MATTER WILL COME

Use these tips for developing travel story ideas over the course of a long-term stay.

By Kristine Jepsen

Mom, are these chocolate chips?" my 10-year-old asked, holding up a bag marked "chispas," its label entirely in Spanish, in what I would call the "expat baking aisle" of la tienda we shopped in Baja California Sur. She was desperate for kid-comfort food, since we'd been south of the U.S. border for a month. But baking actual cookies is a bit of a luxury in most Baja homes, like our rental, because they don't have standard ovens.

By asking around, I discovered that local building practices don't often support the wiring or natural gas lines required for big kitchen appliances, which are also expensive to haul into this out-of-the-way beach community. But the bigger takeaway for me as a writer lay in realizing that chocolate chip cookies represent a non-native food culture, one that takes resources this desert community didn't evolve to support. What if, instead of importing my own expectations, I wondered, I built storylines around how my adopted community works, not just when I've inserted myself, with my deadlines and pitch ideas, but when I'm not?

Here are my go-to practices for finding stories that run deeper than surface details. I've since used my research in Baja to pitch stories to local community newsletters and ex-patriot publications online and in print. I've also used it to caption images made during my stay, sold separately. And of course, my first-hand perspective has informed writing published on my travel blog.

Shop Where the Locals Shop

Not only will you discover shampoo brands that

lather in desalinated sea water, you'll see and hear how families use their resources. In foreign countries, this practice may draw some stares, but you'll quickly figure out when the fish and the fruit are freshest. On one shopping trip, I was tipped off to much-needed garbage pickup—an infrequent and mysterious service that left trash piling up in collection cans—when a young boy came running in with loose change, enough to buy three heavy-gauge plastic trash bags. I asked the cashier why his was so breathless, and she explained the day's expected trash collection route. I would have missed it entirely, likely for another month.

From this exchange, I learned more about the local dump—that it was full and that trash collected traveled 60 miles to a city center for sorting. I started paying better attention to how families broke down and repurposed packaging materials such as plastic milk jugs and composted biodegradable refuse out of necessity, not of environmental conviction. Noticing whose yards were tidy and lush with healthy plants, I began to map out the old-world power structure that got things done in town, a sort of who's who of influence.

Story ideas:

Five Must-Have Toiletries for Desert Travel

Don't Be a Tourist: Handling local currencies

when traveling abroad

Travel Trash: The relationship between tourism and waste management in Baja's beach towns

Go Where the Kids Are

As a parent-writer, one of my biggest needs while traveling is plugging into a social scene not just for myself but for my child. Parents who understand this work-life struggle are often found at playgrounds, waiting at school pickup, walking alongside kids on bikes, and in restaurants right as they open for dinner. Ask them about the challenges facing youth in the community, and you'll likely get good info on schools, the economy, child safety, and local enrichment initiatives, such as a student-run beach clean-up festival.

Story ideas:

Not-So-Public School: How high school education still comes at a cost to Baja families

The Locals Have Landed: Kiteboarding's rising stars are native to its beaches

Investigate Visitor Interests and Concerns

Most destinations have obvious draws: mountains, wildlife, or extreme sports, for example. Another way to get at interesting story material is to ask other visitors about where they come from and why they've made the trip. What are their concerns? In my beach community, the expats had the bead on petty theft of personal property. They also knew how to get Amazon packages delivered (where there's no mail service), set up reliable Internet connectivity, and partner with local landowners to invest in hurricane fortifications for roads and bridges. Professional RV-ers in the main community campground proved to be solar array experts, powering everything from air conditioning to high-voltage blenders. These visitors, who flock to this coastline for its steady wind for kite-boarding and windsurfing, also fundraise year-round for the local ambulance service, which is run 24/7 by a dedicated native resident.

Story ideas:

Coverage vs. Cost: How to map out medical coverage for extreme sports abroad

Business in a Backpack: Ten essentials for setting up a mobile office while traveling

Check Your Bias

I'm not a religious person and often have to remind myself not to overlook religious community when I travel. At the beach, it was at first easy to poke fun at the late-night, open-air hymn-sings hosted by the local evangelical church. Friends and I would make plans to avoid the neighborhood on Saturdays (church night) and warn other newcomers away. But over time, I understood that being friendly with the church-goers—many of the founding families in the community—lent acceptance to my inquiries.

Another sneaky bias is inadaptability to local limitations. If the locals conserve water in how they wash dishes, limit shower time, repurpose waste water for their landscaping, and use local laundry services instead of washing clothes at home, you'd be wise to mimic their accountability to water scarcity. This in turn shows respect for the desert where they've made their home, long before your tenure as a writer-visitor, and long after.

Story ideas:

Laundry is a Luxury: A cold, hard look at wash-water in Baja California Sur

There's a Song in My Soul: Revival sings are still key to Mexican church community

Find the Fun

One of the unsung blessings of traveling with children is that you're subject to their steady chatter and endless questions. The same goes for any place you might land as a writer. Take time to talk to kids (with parents' permission, of course)! Their disarming curiosity will ensure you understand topics at a granular level.

Story ideas:

Don't Flush the Paper! Five kid-friendly tips for travel south of the border

Kids and Salsa: In Mexico, dance is part of most schools' curricula. Here's why we should all learn the language.

Living more like a local takes time—it's not a strategy for a short stay or a press trip. As in parenting, gaining an understanding of a place requires dedication and full contact. My daughter and I bought the chocolate "chispas" that day in the market, but we didn't even try to bake cookies. Instead, we put them in the freezer, and for a week, she parceled them out to a few local kids who wandered over after school, a sort of kid currency. We took the practice home, when we left several weeks later, and now I overhear her explaining to hometown friends how houses are different in Mexico. It's simple knowledge, but it sticks, and for readers and for parent-writers alike, that's the goal, right?

*   *   *

Kristine Jepsen is a grant/writer and farm busi-nessperson in Iowa. Recent nonfiction has won com-petitions at the literary journals Lunch Ticket and

Sweet: A Literary Confection, and appears in Huff-Post, MUTHA Magazine and many others. Her essay, Jaw Wiring: What You Need to Know, is a chapbook. kristinejepsen.com

THE STUMBLING BLOCK: HOW TO FIND UNIQUE STORY ANGLES

When you travel, the thing you stumble over may end up being your secret BFF when it comes to scoring an assignment.

By Judith Fein

When I teach travel writing, I share a secret with my students about how to become a superlative writer by finding unusual story angles. This is more necessary than ever because assignments are hard to come by. Generic pieces go straight from an editor's inbox to trash, and even when you travel to remote places, travel writers have been there before you and written WOW! blogs or articles. So, what's a writer to do?

My secret weapon is what I call The Stumbling Block method. When you are on the road and you encounter any word, visual, event, sign, costume, or activity that is unfamiliar to you, stop. You have just stumbled across something that will lead you to what is unique about a destination. It's easy to nod or shrug or go on with whatever you are doing, but if you stop, just stop, whatever you have stumbled across will lead you where you need to go. It's like a key that opens the door to a unique story angle.

In a town in Mexico, I walked past a window and saw teenage girls and boys in a dancing class; they all – female and male – wore identical bright red skirts. I stopped, stood in front of the window watching, and the teacher waved me inside. It turned out that the teens were being trained to teach Mexican folk dancing to school kids, in order to preserve their culture.

The boys wore the red skirts because they had to be able to teach young girls as well as boys, and they had to experience what it was like to move while wearing a skirt instead of pants. When the class broke, the teacher and his students were excited to tell me about where I could see adults doing the same dances on certain nights. This led to an article about where you can learn Mexican dancing and dance with the locals. And it all started with seeing red skirts.

In Nova Scotia, I was visiting a site that commemorated the cruel 18th century expulsion of Acadians on ships that led them to unknown destinations far away from their families and homes. Husbands and wives were separated. Families were torn apart. Many died at sea. It was a devastating story.

But at this site, I happened to see a man proposing marriage to his girlfriend, and a young couple who were proudly bringing their toddler along. It seemed so incongruous to me.

Instead of being sad, they seemed buoyant. Why would you celebrate happy occasions or bring your baby to such a tragic place? I stopped. I waited until there was an opportune moment to speak to the newly engaged couple and the young parents, and the result was a revelation for me and a subsequent chapter in a book about Acadians' proud celebration of their survival.

Matera, Italy, was unknown to the rest of the world before World War II when Carlo Levi, a doctor, painter, writer, and activist was exiled there for his anti-fascist activities. When he arrived, he was horrified at the poverty and conditions the people lived in. They inhabited caves with their animals, with no amenities or social services.

As a result of a book he wrote about it, there was a forced evacuation of the population of troglodytes in the area, as their living spaces were considered uninhabitable. They were resettled in the modern city.

Today, Matera is internationally famous for the achingly beautiful historic region called the Sassi; many of the caves have been transformed into restaurants, shops, and even luxury hotels.

The manager of the cave I was staying in mentioned that some of the original evacuees were still around. That did it. I stopped. I HAD to meet them. They were a living history. I was like a dog chasing a bone until the manager agreed to invite two of them to the cave hotel.

They were quite friendly, very unpretentious, and they opened up about what their life was like when they lived in a cave and after they left. I assumed that they were grateful for being moved to hygienic housing, but what was surprising was that they were also nostalgic for their life in the cave. Why? That's exactly what I wrote about.

On a cruise ship plying Russian waters, I was discussing the best vodkas with two Siberian bartenders. We were laughing and joking, and one of them referred to "a vodka with an ordinary name that is really great. It's what the Mafia drinks." I saw a big stop sign. What made it so great? Why did the Russian Mafia choose it? It led to a two-hour conversation about vodka culture, and it also led to an unusual insider story about vodka from the Siberian pros.

Perhaps, as you read these examples, you understand the concept of stumbling blocks, and why they lead to unusual story angles. But you may also feel uncomfortable about talking to strangers and asking them questions.

The last secret is that people love to talk about what they do, how they do it, their culture, foods, beliefs, lives. Even people who are generally laconic become talkative when they are speaking about the way they live. But they will generally only open up if they find that you are really interested in them. And how does this manifest? You listen, you pay attention, you ask relevant questions, you smile, you become vulnerable, and you open up about yourself, too. They see that you care and they are willing to share.

Talking and listening to people and caring about

them is the best way to find meaningful, unique, resonant stories. Almost everyone you meet has a potential story or can lead you to one with a fascinating angle. It's your job to pick up the clues, explore, and discover the story.

Now start stumbling!

* * *

Judith Fein is an award-winning travel and culture journalist, author, and speaker who lives to leave. She has contributed to 110 publications, blogs about Transformative Travel for Psychology Today, and gave an acclaimed TEDx talk about Deep Travel. Her newest book is How To Communicate With The Dead...and How Cultures Do It Around the World. Her website is www.GlobalAdventure.us.

HOW TO THINK OUTSIDE OF TRAVEL (AND EARN MORE MONEY AS A RESULT)

Travel writing parallels travelling in so many ways - you can only land a hidden gem if you go off the beaten track.

By Qin Xie

As a freelance travel writer, the travel sections of newspapers, magazines, and websites are normally your first port of call when looking for inspiration, or researching your next trip, or hunting for potential editors to pitch. But should they be?

Dwindling budgets and hobby writers willing to submit free copy have made the industry horribly competitive. Which means it is appropriate to ask the question: could I earn more by pitching other kinds of work?

Broadly speaking, I find there are two types of travel writers - the ones who are primarily based at home and the ones who are constantly on the road. How you approach this horizon-broadening strategy will depend on which of these profiles you fit best.

Home-based travel writers

It might be counterintuitive to think of a travel writer as being based at home, but it is possible.

I've worked in-house on the travel sections of a number of UK nationals, and the majority of the original stories were sourced right from the office.

Yes! I was a desk-bound travel writer.

When you think about it, most profile or interview pieces can be done remotely, via Skype, phone, or email. Then, it's just a case of sourcing images or video to go with the interview. So, do you really need to take three days out of your schedule to meet one person?

In-flight magazines can be some of the best outlets to place these non-travel features. Most will cover a broad spectrum of subjects, including news, restaurant reviews, celebrity profiles, entertainment, art and culture and more, as long as there is a hook that ties the story to the destination where the airline flies.

Reading widely can help as well. Spotting a new journal article on climate change could be the news hook you need to pitch a feature on eco-friendly resorts to a women's magazine, for example, or a piece on how these resorts may not be all they're cracked up to be.

A new tourist tax being introduced in another country could spark a comment piece for a national newspaper on whether they should be introduced in your own country. Or it could turn into a news analysis feature on how different nations are combating over-tourism. For a travel trade publication, this could be a piece on how to overcome anti-tourism sentimentality.

Social media can be another great resource for

stories, especially if you're pitching to news-papers. A travel influencer with a great back-story could make a stunning photo-led profile piece for a website. Holidaymakers' complaints about food poisoning could turn into a strong holiday nightmares piece, with good photos and evidence to back it up. And insider tips spot-ted in a private Facebook group might just shape into a practical money-saving piece for a con-sumer section.

Don't forget, many news outlets around the world have a global outlook. If there's a story with national interest around you, it just might work for the world section of a newspaper based elsewhere.

One spa writer I know living in an area that was suddenly hit with weeks of political protests managed to win commissions for hard news stories. Always be open to opportunity, even if it doesn't fit inside your regular beat.

Just bear in mind, most editors will look for an angle that's relatable to their readers. So, a story about an Australian expat living in the United States might work better for an Australian news-paper than a British one, for example.

On-the-road travel writers

Being constantly on the road can be exhausting, but it can lead to some great stories.

But one mistake that many writers make, especially if they've come from a print background, is that they're too focused on the words. For a commissioning editor, visualizing how the story can be told via images or graphics is hugely important, especially for websites. So, think about what else you could bring to the table.

If you're on a trip, you want to maximize your time by getting as many commissions and stories out of it as possible. The one advantage you have over home-based writers is that you're on the ground and can source additional content.

Spotting a new fashion trend and having the photographs to go with it could turn into an exclusive piece in a fashion magazine. And even if it doesn't turn into a feature, your photographs could be sold via stock or specialist agencies such as Getty and Alamy.

If you're in the right place to film a bizarre weather phenomenon or even a weird bug, a short video can make you a nice fee if sold to an agency or news outlet. Think about the sorts of things that make viral videos and look out for them. And don't forget audio - these could be sold to radio or podcast.

It's not just about different formats of storytelling, either. You should think about the different contexts where your story could work.

I've been on a food-led trip with someone who managed to sell a preview feature to the arts section of a newspaper - and all it took was two hours out of the itinerary to meet the curator of a show. Similarly, another freelancer I know turned a visit to a winery into features for a design magazine and a profile piece for a business magazine.

If you're feeling constantly jetlagged, there might be a health feature in it on new ways to combat the condition. And don't forget trade or business magazines, which are always hungry for profiles and trends pieces.

So if there is one piece of advice I'd like to leave, it is this: forget about your run-of-the-mill, "what I did on my holiday"-type travel pieces.

Yes, they make great bylines, and marketers will love you for them. But they're not nearly as lucrative as they need to be for you to make a living.

Instead, think about how you can maximize your time, whether at home or away.

* * *

Qin Xie is a London-based journalist and editor specializing in food and travel. She has worked on na-

tional newspapers in the UK and has written for international publications including CNN, Conde Nast Traveller, and Lonely Planet.

THE FUTURE OF TRAVEL WRITING

The writing world has changed dramatically in recent years. To make sure your stories are fresh and relevant in this new era of travel writing, you need to tailor your approach accordingly.

By Elyse Hauser

The dust in the writing industry is still settling from the massive overhaul caused by the advent of the internet. Travel writing wasn't spared from this shakeup. And if there's one thing travel writers can learn from this shift, it's that the ability to pivot quickly and respond to changing trends is essential for success.

So what does an aspiring travel writer need to prepare for next? Although shifting trends are never perfectly predictable, a few things are clear. Here's how to make sure your writing stays interesting, relevant, and marketable in this changing landscape.

Write for a Global Audience

Thanks to the internet, it's more important than ever to write for an audience of multiple cultures and many different backgrounds. Writers must be sensitive to how personal perspectives and culture color their experiences, and avoid sounding ignorant or offensive (even unintentionally so). A single culturally insensitive comment can become a career-ender if it makes enough rounds online.

Travel writers from Europe and the U.S. should take care to avoid Eurocentrism, or the perspective that Western cultures are the "norm" and other cultures are unusual or odd. "Poverty tourism," or visiting impoverished areas to express shock at the misfortune of their residents, should also be avoided. This doesn't mean disadvantaged parts of the world aren't excellent candidates for travel articles. However, it does mean that writers should cultivate sensitivity to the global politics and history that creates poverty in a region.

For example, as an outsider, pitching a story called "The Harsh Realities of Life in Brazil's Favelas" is best avoided. But a pitch titled "The Thriving Art Scene Within Brazil's Favelas" offers a fresh perspective that doesn't rely on poverty tourism. Write respectfully about other cultures and people, and avoid stories that hinge solely on shock value or romanticization. Always keep in mind that the people reading your work might come from backgrounds wildly different from your own.

Build a Meta Perspective

Today's travel writers can increasingly enjoy the benefits of working nomadically. You no longer have to report back to an office in a specific city: you can just as easily make your "office" by the beach in Bali or at a Parisian cafe.

This industry shift provides a wealth of writing potential. You can build wonderfully self-referential stories that offer a window into the experience of a "digital nomad," or you can write about how this shift has affected the world of work on the whole. Pitches like "What My First Year as a Remote Worker Taught Me" or "How Coworking Spaces Have Revolutionized Work" offer a compelling way to tie your personal experiences into the bigger picture of travel, writing, and work.

Consider the Environment

As the climate continues to change across the globe, it will become increasingly impossible for even the most casual travelers to ignore. While climate change doesn't need to be a focal point of every travel article, it will play a bigger role in the travel writing of the future.

As you choose destinations and pitch stories, it's wise to be sensitive to how ecological issues could impact your story (or play a role in telling it completely). There's also a wellspring of new topics that tie this global issue to the experience in a specific location.

For example, modern readers are often interested in learning how to travel without negatively impacting the environment. You could pitch "10 Ecofriendly Questions to Ask Yourself Before Your Next Vacation" or "How Tourism Threatens Bali's Natural Beauty" to captivate this audience.

Understand Content Marketing Opportunities

Content marketing, or inserting mentions of specific brands into otherwise informative writing, has become an increasingly reliable way for writers to pay the bills. While content marketing raises certain ethical questions, it does have the potential to bring new opportunities to the travel writer's table.

For example, if you rely heavily on a certain product when you travel, you might want to reach out to the brand to see if you can forge a partnership. They may be willing to pay you for sharing "affiliate links" to their products. Then, you can work the links into informative pieces with titles like "The New Tech Tools You Should Never Leave Home Without."

Content marketing works best if you only name-drop brands and products that you truly stand behind. Taking any and all brand partnerships that you're offered can weaken your reputation if readers discover that not every product you mention is really up to par. But when approached with care, content marketing might be a handy way to supplement your travel writing income.

Keep Mobile Tech in Mind

Today's readers often view content on smartphones and tablets, not laptops. This change in format means dense or long-form writing can quickly become overwhelming to the eye.

For example, a lack of paragraph breaks or white space might lead readers on smartphones to click away quickly. Keep the mobile audience in mind as you write. Consider using shorter paragraphs to add more relaxing white space to the page (breaking up large blocks of text with attractive images also works well). And remember that short-form reads can be just as valuable as long, detailed ones.

While you may not always have the power to choose how your writing gets formatted for publication, you will write differently when you're sensitive to how readers consume your work.

Also, keep in mind that many readers will now find your work via social media on their mobile devices. Your articles must stand out to readers scrolling quickly through a site. A catchy lede and compelling title can help you get more clicks, which will keep your clients coming back for more.

Try Multimedia Work

The popularity of social media and mobile tech also means that people want different kinds of content. Writing still does well in these spaces, but it can do even better when supplemented with great images or video stories.

Consider learning the basics of photography, or teaching yourself to make travel videos that people will want to share online. Thanks to smartphones, you no longer need expensive equipment to hone these skills. Publications often hire writers that have multimedia skills before they hire ones that can only write. And these talents can also help you build a bigger following independently, such as on your own travel blog.

Dig Deeper

Social media can create a feedback loop in which trendy stories quickly become tired. For the travel writers of the future, it won't be enough to simply follow the content trends: you'll need to be able to dig deeper and provide an interesting perspective on what everyone's already talking about.

For example, the "farm-to-table" dining concept has been popular for several years, making it a tired topic. While you may be able to publish a piece about farm-to-table dining in a certain city, that piece won't stand out from the crowd of similar ones. But if you dig deeper, it will.

To dig deeper, you could seek to answer why today's travelers love the farm-to-table idea so much, with a pitch like "How Farm-to-Table Dining Went from Trend to Tradition." Or, you could explore whether there's any accountability for restaurants that claim to offer a farm-to-table experience. While not every travel piece you write needs to be deep and philosophical, digging deeper into topics creates a valuable source of truly unique content ideas.

To thrive in the future of travel writing, your

content must resonate even among the noise of the internet's constant publishing stream. The industry's changes can feel unpredictable and hard to keep up with at times. But if you keep your finger on the pulse of these trends, you'll set yourself up for success for years to come.

* * *

Elyse Hauser is a Seattle-based writer and editor with a Master's in Writing Studies from Saint Joseph's University. Her work has appeared in publications like Racked, Vine Leaves Literary Journal, and Rum Punch Press, and she was awarded a 2017 Writing Between the Vines residency. When she's not writing, she's exploring her passions for dance, travel, fashion, and history. Learn more at elysehauser.com.

HOW TO WRITE WITH MEANING, IMPACT AND PERSONALITY

FOREWORD BY KIM LAMBERT

When you read a book or an article, do you think about how well it's written, how well the author uses language? It is almost certain that you don't. Unless, of course, it is badly written and it spoils your reading experience.

As a writer, it is imperative that you write well enough to allow your readers to forget they are reading!

As a travel writer, it is, in some ways, even more important than it is for someone writing a novel, or a 'how to' book. Why? Because travel writing is all about emotion and experience, about making the person feel like they are there, or want to be there. And most travel articles are fairly short, so a jarring experience probably means the reader will simply stop reading, and will lose an emotional connection with the words.

This section of this book is all about the craft of travel writing – ways to improve the reader experience, and ways that you can bring something different to your work, which engages readers and makes your work stand out.

From start to finish, you'll find something here to help you improve and polish that article perfectly.

We cover:

1. **Bringing a distinctive voice** and authenticity to your writing (so that the reader feels like you are their best friend, recommending their next journey)

2. **Profiling people** in new and interesting ways, beyond the basic interview (every person you ever meet when you travel could represent an intriguing article)

3. Ways to create **unusual types of articles**, to draw the reader into a location, or to help them find those hidden local gems when travelling (step beyond the listicle forever!)

4. Discovering new ways to **align your writing with your photography** (so that editors love the 'whole package' that you bring to them)

5. **The basics** of getting your writing right (all of that spelling and grammar that tortured you at school suddenly becomes useful!)

So read on, and prepare to transform your travel writing forever.

* * *

Kim Lambert is a speaker, photographer, writing and publishing Coach, a travel writer and a multi-time Amazon bestselling author, with more than 70 books published to date. She is also the owner of a publishing company, Dreamstone Publishing, which publishes books for a variety of authors, and also works with other large publishing companies to enhance and update their current catalogues for digital book delivery.

THE IMPORTANCE OF YOUR TRAVEL WRITING 'VOICE'

Why does authenticity matter in your travel writing – and what does 'authenticity' really mean? Authenticity allows people to connect with what you have written. And that emotional connection works best when you develop your own unique 'voice' and style of writing.

By Sandra Henriques

A couple of years ago I was interviewing the marketing representative of a travel startup and he, disheartened, confessed how disappointed he was with the online travel content he was seeing. He said, and I'm paraphrasing, "The top ten results on the first page of search engines aren't the best articles; they're just the websites with the best SEO [search engine optimization] techniques."

He needed to feel the connection to a destination through someone's writing, more than he needed to know the top things to see and do. He wanted to know about the backstreet restaurants that guidebooks don't include, and the small shops that tourists don't generally know about. In a nutshell, he wanted the true 'off the beaten track' information, not the same commonly presented information just wrapped up in a different way.

It takes more than an internet connection to put you in touch with an audience. Anyone can whip up a top ten list of what to see in a destination, but it takes hard work to convey a message, a true sense of a place. The ultimate guides and must-see lists this marketing representative was coming across lacked soul, despite the tone of the content being generally witty and upbeat.

Sometimes too positive, in fact, and yet without reflecting the locations in a way that made him want to visit.

Authentic travel writing makes readers understand there are people at a destination. That the place they're visiting is not just a product on their tour package. That, for better or for worse, they have an impact on someone else's lives and this is crucial at a time when the travel industry is plagued by one case of 'overtourism' after another. Even if the reader doesn't travel at all, they should learn from the article that there's a story about the destination beyond sightseeing.

So – how do you achieve that authenticity, that connection with the reader? Here are four steps to help you create authenticity in your writing, and you'll notice that it's 75 percent preparation and only 25 percent actual writing:

Step 1: Finding your voice = knowing your audience
Step 2: Finding the story (and stepping out of the spotlight)
Step 3: Select. Observe. Take notes. Repeat.
Step 4: Writing, at last! (Setting the scene and giving context)

Step 1: Finding Your Voice = Knowing Your Audience

Be yourself sounds like a lazy piece of advice,

but that's what your author voice should be. When I started out in travel writing, I followed dozens of paths and tips on how to do it. The results were disastrous, a clump of forced articles that had nothing to do with me because that voice was someone else's.

You can't, and you shouldn't, write for everyone.

Writing is a lonely task, especially when you're starting out and you don't have an audience. So, defining an ideal reader persona helps you focus on your style. You can build more than one persona (and give them names), or you can tweak your persona as your style evolves or you focus on a different topic within travel writing. That way, you are writing directly for that imaginary person – and for any person you imagine, there will be millions just like them out there in the real world.

Unless you're on assignment for a client who has a set style guide, you should always be writing for your persona, mentally bouncing your ideas off them. I don't mean 'write and the readers will come', I mean write for the specific readers you want to reach.

Step 2: Finding The Story (And Stepping Out Of The Spotlight)

If you're waiting for inspiration to hit when you reach your destination and you think you can wing it, you're being naïve at best and amateurish at worst.

The first thing to do before traveling is to read all of the content you possibly can about the destination. Blogs, magazines, books, different authors and different times. Gather as many perspectives as you can. Challenge whatever preconceptions you have of your destination. Look for the passing mentions of things you've never heard about before, then go digging deeper to discover more.

Researching a destination or a new angle will, many times, have you tumbling down the research rabbit hole. At one point, you might even feel like that destination has been fully covered. What else can you write if it feels like someone has written everything possible already? Well, that's the time when you have to let the story find you.

Leave for your destination with a safety cushion list of topics you'd like to write about, but arrive with an open mind. Whatever allows you to feel the pulse of your destination, use it - the conversation with the taxi driver on the way to your hotel, asking the receptionist for suggestions of local dishes, going on a small group cultural tour for three hours.

Use whatever material those moments give you to include as an anecdote in your main story, or to give context to a top tourist attraction. Weave it in so your article doesn't feel flat, you don't want it to come across as having been written by someone who went there to do the same thing thousands of people have done before.

As a travel writer, it's okay to be in and out of the story, but we shouldn't make it about us. To be authentic and let your voice come through, you don't have to talk about yourself all the time. Think of yourself as a sort of stage director. You show up to set the scene and introduce the characters, step out to narrate the scene that's unfolding, come in again to add a new detail or a secondary character, and so forth.

Unless it's an episode worth telling because it reveals something about the destination, it's pointless to describe how long it took for you to get to baggage claim, for example. Is it a practical detail that needs to be addressed and that somehow impacted your arrival? Fine to mention, but make it snappy.

Step 3: Select. Observe. Take Notes. Repeat.

Every text or photo can be tweaked later, but that first, raw impression of a place is unique, whether it's your first or your tenth time there. Most travel writers won't see a destination more than once, though. Therefore, more than detailing the dates or time of year we visited, we need to recount the destination as it was when we saw it.

To convey authenticity, you can't rush through a destination. Take one day to just sit at a busy part of town, preferably where locals go, not tourists, observe and take notes. There is so much you can feel from a destination just by watching how people go about their daily routines. No matter how clichéd this sounds, this is the soul of a place that a travel reader is eager to know about. Anyone can give information about what bus to take around town, but whatever happened in the bus when you took it is unique.

Return to the same spot on different days and at different times, or as many times as you can. If you have limited time, write an extra set of notes from memory the next morning. You'll notice some images stuck for you and others didn't, and it helps you weed out what would probably be fluff.

Always take note of the things that affect your physical senses – what can you see? What can you hear? What can you smell? What does the food or drink taste like? Are there unique textures to the place, things that you touch? Adding descriptions of things like that into your writing helps the reader truly imagine being there.

A personal note on taking notes: smartphones and laptops became more than a work tool, they're an extension of us. I find that taking notes on my smartphone is not as effective as writing things down in a notebook. Partly because writing on paper shields me from the urge of snapping a shot with my phone and adding it as a visual aid to my notes. The point is to not have visual aids. The point is to see if and how you can set the scene using only words.

Step 4: Writing, At Last! (Setting The Scene And Giving Context)

When I was reading Paul Theroux's 'Riding the Iron Rooster', it was almost like being on the train with him. He steps in and out of the story as needed, as someone who once in a while whispers something in your ear to set the scene that unfolds before your eyes. Occasionally, he gives context to stories and people with political and historical facts. The reader is able to see most of China in just a few sentences.

Travel writing doesn't have to be bluntly political, but it should acknowledge how some events have shaped that destination. Giving readers and potential travelers cultural and historical context about a destination is your job, but keep it light. Think of it as an add-on.
Your articles need to paint a picture, even if the reader chooses to focus only on one corner of the frame.

It doesn't matter if you're writing a two-day itinerary that covers the top attractions or you're staying a month in your destination, you must bring the reader with you:

Write an opening paragraph that conveys the time of day and what the place feels like (sight, sound, smell etc);

Keep practical information to a minimum (some authors or publications choose to include them in a paragraph at the bottom of the article, or in a sidebar), and focus on conveying a sense of space;

Weave in relevant episodes that are happening around you;

At all times, keep in mind the story you want to tell.

Consider – how do you want the reader to feel, after reading your story? Do you want them to feel as if they've been there? Or instantly want to book a trip to that destination?

If you follow these four steps, you will find your own authentic voice naturally, over the course of a few articles – and the people who read those articles will be happier as a result.

❧ ❧ ❧

Sandra Henriques Gajjar is a Portuguese freelance

web content writer born in the Azores Islands and based in Lisbon. She also writes about travel, culture, and the people she meets in between at her blog Tripper.pt, where she's an advocate for sustainable cultural tourism.

WRITING ABOUT PEOPLE: BEYOND THE INTERVIEW

Always remember, travel writing doesn't have to just be about places. Sometimes it should also be about the people you meet.

By Diana Plater

When we travel, often what we remember most strongly is the people we meet – people we may never see again, but who are a key part of what makes our travel experience wonderful. Yet in travel writing, we often forget to write about those people. There are plenty of interview-based articles out there, focusing on the famous or important people, but not much at all looking at people as we observe and interact with them.

So let's look at the potential for articles that fill this niche, whether they are about well-known people, or simply the taxi driver or guide you met on a trip, and how to craft them.

Well-known travel writer Pico Iyer has said the allure of travel writing for many people is "that they can throw fiction and nonfiction and every-thing in between into their narratives". The art is to use fiction writing skills but not, of course, to actually write fiction when it comes to pro-files.

The Interviewless Profile

Not all profiles are based on interviews, and while it is usually preferable to interview your subject, it's not always possible. Or you may be more interested in painting a picture of a subject without their words coming into it. Whatever the case, you should aim at building a colourful but accurate portrait of a person.

Case Study:

An article written by Gay Talese for The Esquire, Frank Sinatra Has a Cold, is perhaps the best and definitely the most famous account of a person where the writer observed his subject but never interviewed him. Frank Sinatra Has a Cold - Gay

Talese - Best Profile of Sinatra - Esquire.

In this story, which weaves background information, interviews with others and descriptions of scenes and dialogue, Talese builds up a
portrait of the singer in a pioneering example of
a new form of writing that came to be known as
New Journalism.

The article, which ran in April 1966, has been
described as 'rigorously faithful fact enlivened
with the kind of vivid storytelling that had previously been reserved for fiction'.
For those wanting to write about the characters
they have met during their travels, the Talese
piece is worth studying.

There are many different ways to approach
doing an interviewless profile, but firstly, the
most important is to keenly observe your subject, his or her environment and the surrounding
people.
Research is naturally important. It can be based
on previously published profiles of the subject,
public commentary, reportage, and interviews
with others. While Wikipedia is helpful for a
well-known person, make sure you check other
sources too.

Mini biographies give the facts about the subject's life, work or family. Insert factual information as it becomes relevant, not in one long
block.

You can quote from emails or phone conversations if you have taken notes or face-to-face conversations that aren't interviews. Include anecdotes that reveal something about the person, they really lift a story. They can be stories that the subject has told you or stories others have told about him or stories about the two of you together. They can be based on memories of the subject or those close to him or can be used to back up your own observations.

Snatches of conversation – if you get the quotes absolutely correct – can also enhance a story as can be seen in the Sinatra tale.

Writing Your Article

Be descriptive. Attention to detail is important. You can also be analytical about the person's behaviour. Have you observed their body language? What did you think of him or her?

If you have met the person your article focuses on, then you can describe how you met and what you did, what your first observations were. This is known as scene setting and can be good opening material. This is sometimes in the present tense, after which a past tense account takes over, often beginning with the short background account of the subject's past.

Sometimes it helps to focus on an object. For example, I once did a profile on a 90-year-old former ballerina, Anna Volkova. The photographer I was working with asked if she had any old ballet shoes from when she used to dance for the Ballet Russes. She smiled shyly and said they were in a box at the top of her cupboard. The photographer climbed on top of a chair and got them down and then took photos of her holding them. The ballet shoes were the lead in to the story. To quote from the story:

> 'Volkova carries out a plastic box of old photos, showing her dancing in several ballets and one of her at the age of 13 wearing her first pointe shoes.

> 'But her biggest treasure is hidden away in a box at the top of a bedroom wardrobe. It's the battered and worn pink ballet slippers she wore when the company of 19 nationalities was holed up in Buenos Aires during World War 2 at a time when they couldn't afford silk ribbons and they had to make shoes last as long as possible.

> '...In fact, they're the last pair of ballet shoes she ever wore for the Ballet Russes company or any other.'

You can describe what they're wearing but make sure it's relevant to the story. Don't just give a boring description. How do the clothes reflect the person's personality? In your physical description look for the telling detail rather than everything they have on.

As in the Sinatra article:

> 'He was, as usual, immaculately dressed. He wore an oxford-grey suit with a vest, a suit conservatively cut on the outside but trimmed with flamboyant silk within; his shoes, British, seemed to be shined even on the bottom of the soles. He also wore, as everybody seemed to know, a remarkably convincing black hairpiece, one of sixty that he owns.'

By focusing on your subject's background and personal history, you have the opportunity to write about related social or cultural issues, and this can be more meaningful in the broader context of where they live, their home, their family, community and so on. Which leads us to the next type of people focussed writing.

Stories based on 'ordinary people'

When you travel, you meet people, continuously. Hotel receptionists and staff, taxi drivers, local travel guides, shopkeepers and more. Each of those people, and the tasks they deal with in daily life, is a potential story in the making.

For example, stories about travel guides and how they've enlivened people's experiences can bring a place to life. In Rajasthan, India, our guide was a member of the Rajput, or warrior class. He told me funny stories of his mother trying to find a wife for him of the same class, and that sort of detail enhanced the article I wrote and helped readers to understand the culture and history.

It makes a much better piece when you can interview members of the subject's family or friends or workmates, whoever is relevant to the theme of the story. This provides background and contrasting views of the person, and quotes. When they are used, they need to be attributed clearly, without disrupting the flow.

Case Study:

I wrote a story about an Aboriginal traditional owner in the Kimberley in far north-west Australia, who was the subject of a documentary directed by his great nephew. I didn't formally interview him but chatted with him and wrote down some of his comments and what he told people. I observed him and what others said about him. I wrote about how his great nephew first met him as a way of explaining the then government policies of taking Aboriginal children away from their parents and communities. (The director's mother was a member of what is known as the Stolen Generations.)

I set the scene by describing the heat and the country we were travelling in:

'It's the calm before the storm -- the intense heat that builds up before the beginning of the wet season.

'We're about two hours' drive north of the Aboriginal community of Yiyili in the Kimberley region of Western Australia.

'The vehicles we're travelling in are feeling the heat as much as we are with screaming fan belts and bubbling radiators.

'...But senior Lunga Kitja and Gooniyandi man Matt Pagey Dawson is determined to show us his country -- the waterholes, birth trees, sand soaks, caves, gorges and dry river-beds fringed with wulladi -- white gums -- of the Mueller Ranges, part of Louisa Downs, an Aboriginal-owned cattle station around 100km west of Halls Creek.'

The story uses travel writing techniques to portray Indigenous history, language and culture through the story of Matt Dawson.

Have a look at the way obituaries are written. They often include quotes from other people, or anecdotes that add context, as well as background. If you are writing about somebody you know well, then you can include your own memories of times you shared together.

For a blog about an Indonesian musician who

had recently died, I focused on his widow.

> 'She served us chilled water as she told us one of the saddest stories I've ever heard...of how she took him to hospital, where he died a month later from complications of diabetes.

> 'She played us clips of Erin singing Eric Clapton's Wonderful Tonight and another song he wrote for her. He was about to record an album and his career was really taking off.

> '"He always sang with his heart," she said.'

If you have a large amount of technical material, or a complex timeline of events associated with the person, and needing to be presented for the reader, that can be provided as a side-bar or break-out box, or via an embedded link.

While it's common to write in the first person, be wary of inserting yourself between the reader and the subject.

Key Points

Most readers are not that interested in the writer, they want to know about the subject and location – something I feel emerging travel writers should be deeply aware of. Especially in a people focussed article, concentrate on things that will make the person come to life in the mind of the reader – so not just a collection of dry details listing their achievements, but a description of the small things about them, that make the reader think 'they are a person, just like me, but with different experiences'. Those things create empathy, and make the article far more enjoyable for the reader.

You can create an article about anyone – every person has things about them, which they think are ordinary, but which others will think are extraordinary – find those things!

* * *

Diana Plater is an Australian travel writer, journalist and author, who has reported internationally, including from Latin America and the USA. Her novel, Whale Rock, won the Gold award for Popular Literary Fiction in the Global Ebook Awards, 2019. Her play, Havana, Harlem, is about Fidel Castro in New York in 1960. www.diana-plater.com

HOW TO WRITE 'UNUSUAL' ARTICLES

Finding a new way to tell the story of a place – a way that potential visitors can easily engage with - will set your pitch apart from run-of-the-mill articles.

By Rachael Rowe

Here are three examples of different article types you might create, which leverage all of the information you would usually collect about a location, but present it in a new and interesting way.

Walking Guides

Exploring a city or region on foot is increasingly

popular, and a self-guided trail is usually free. It's also good exercise and your article is as likely to be used by locals as tourists. Your article needs to be compelling to a local person or second time visitor, to give them the inspiration to get out and walk. There are some crucial things a walking guide writer needs to consider, before putting pen to paper. Planning is vital. Without having made these decisions, and gathered the information, you can't compile it into an effective guide.

- How long is the walk?
- Is it linear or circular?
- How difficult is the terrain?
- Has the walk got a spectacular viewpoint or is it themed around an interesting local character? What makes it interesting enough that someone will want to do it?
- Who is your audience? Is the walk aimed at families, or seasoned hikers?
- How accessible is the walk to people on mobility scooters?

As a rough guide, a circular walk up to five miles is suitable for most families, whereas experienced hikers will be looking for something more challenging. Most town and city walks are up to three miles.

I always walk every step of the walks I write about - and sometimes I have walked the trails three or four times to get the route perfect. I cannot emphasize enough the importance of doing this part of the work personally on foot. Do not rely on online sources using Google Maps or similar. Places change and your reader will not thank you for sending them on a walk that ends up at a blocked route. When writing one of my walking guides to Devon, England I followed what I believed to be a marked trail along a river - only to find the entire path eroded from major floods - and the only way through was to turn back. Another time, what I thought would be a simple road crossing turned out to be a really busy major route too dangerous for walkers.

When you are walking the route, make notes and take photos. This helps you remember the steps for your write up. Walks must be on public land only. They should not cross private premises unless a public trailway or footpath traverses the property and is marked as a permissive route. Check any potential hazards such as a steep slope or a walk affected by tidal flows. I also note any cafes, toilets, and car parks in the area as this is useful information for walkers when planning their day. Stiles and gates are vital to note as they affect people with limited abilities or those with pushchairs.

Including a map is an option and adds clarity to the walk. Many map companies operate under license and so you will need a permit to use their maps in your work. An alternative is to draw a map. I always add reference details of a standard map such as Ordnance Survey to the information panel and geo coordinates of the start and finish so that walkers can plan the route.

Give very clear instructions when writing your walk. What seems obvious to you can appear ambiguous to others. Once you have written your guide, check it for accuracy before submitting it to an editor. Testing it out will also give you an idea of how easy that walk is to follow and whether you need to do further refinements.

Cycling Articles

Cycling is increasingly popular. Articles that work well are those featuring long distance routes, classic cycling trails, and destination features with options for using two wheels. New cycle routes in an area are also topical feature material. As with the walking guides, it is vital to have tested out and be familiar with these trails and not just rely on an internet map or description. You will need to consider who the article is pitched at and how easy or challenging the route is.

Is this a trail suitable for families or mature cyclists, or is it focused on those who do time trials at weekends?

The terrain is important to include as this not only impacts the skills and ability of the cyclist but affects the bike they will be using. There is a significant difference between using paved cycle paths and off-road hillsides. Clear directions are vital, particularly for those going off road.

Increasingly, people are using electronic bikes which can be challenging to transport. Others don't want to bring a conventional bicycle with them but do want to explore an area by bike. Check out any rental companies that can be listed in your practical information guide. Some cities have rental bikes as part of their transportation system which may be relevant to your article. You will need to make or record notes and take photos as part of your research and write up. Always take more photos and notes than you think you will need, as it is useful reference material. The good news about cycling is that it is becoming so popular, that these articles are not just limited to cycle magazines, but can be sold to more general publications as well.

Anniversary Articles

Focusing an article on a special anniversary of a significant event is another way to create interesting features. This ranges from the centenary of a business to the anniversary of a famous person's birth or death, where that person is associated with various locations. When writing these types of articles, planning is essential. Your ideas need to be created around two years to eighteen months ahead. This gives you sufficient time to develop and create your outline and pitch it to an editor well in advance of the event itself. Don't forget to work backwards from the event itself to an editor's planning meeting and publication schedule. Add in your pitch and writing time and in some cases you will need to be working two years ahead of the pack to get your ideas in on time.

Special events such as D Day commemorations or the 500th anniversary of the death of Leonardo Da Vinci are planned years in advance and have significant media coverage. Several newspapers and magazines work in collaboration with tourism boards to maximise visitor footfall during the anniversary. This means that as a freelancer you should be looking for unusual perspectives to the story that differ from the mainstream events promoted by the tourist board. Having a stand out unique view sets you apart from other freelancers. Do your research well in advance of the event to find out those unusual angles such as alternative cities associated with a famous person or a first-person interview to add context to a place. Do collaborate with tourism boards to develop your story. Most are really helpful and will support you with information and useful contact details of people to interview.

Some anniversary events are not well known

but a well- researched article gives a reason to visit an area and highlight some of the lesser known facts about a region. A recent example that stood out for me included an article to mark the centenary of a local cider making business in Somerset, England. It drew attention to the industry and was an excellent reason to visit that area. Another was a 50-year anniversary of a song set in Berlin which presented a unique dimension to the city. With anniversaries you can be really creative and celebrate all manner of obscure events to highlight an aspect of a destination. These articles work well in newspapers, in-flight magazines, and even some regional publications.

So – now that you have seen some examples – what creative article types can you envision? Always look for the chance to write something different about a location – the more angles you can bring to a place, the more articles you can produce from a single trip.

❊ ❊ ❊

Rachael Rowe is a travel and health writer from Dorset, England. She has authored walking guides and guidebooks and writes for online and print publications.

SNAP FIRST, WRITE SECOND: HOW TO USE PHOTOGRAPHY TO GUIDE YOUR ARTICLE

As a travel writer who also takes photos of the places you write about, how do you let your best shots guide you in terms of what you write, so that the final package is irresistible to editors?

By Wayne Moran

In a previous section of this book, we discussed why good photography matters. We're not going to rehash that information – I'm going to assume that you've got that down. My purpose here is to help you write the best articles you can, to leverage the great shots I'm going to assume you've taken.

I am a fine art travel photographer, even more than a writer. So, I am always looking for that amazing iconic image which makes people sit back and say, "Wow! I want to travel there!"

If you are like me, you have probably taken way too many images, so your first step in the process is to whittle down your list of images to the best of the best. I know it's hard, but you must do it. Have a friend or family member work with you, so that you can see how the images are affecting people other than just yourself. You must be ruthless with this process to get to the best.

Now that you have five to ten of your best images, let's start the crafting process of the actual story. The next step is to consider very carefully who your audience is. With that focus, how will you craft a story that will move the most people?

For example, if you are writing for a hiking

magazine, you would be writing the technical details of the hike to get you to the place where you could take this amazing image.

If you were writing for a photography magazine, you would write the technical details related to how to capture that perfect image. This could include details about the camera, the lens, camera configuration, time of day, etc.

If you were writing an article about traveling in Florence Italy, you would craft the article around either seeing the most iconic places, or maybe finding all the hidden gems that no one else knows about.

Can you see how knowing your audience is critical here?

Let's run through each of these examples to see how the story writing process is different.

Hiking Magazine

In a hiking magazine, your article will be focused on what a hiker wants to know. What are the types of things that a hiker would want to know so that they can easily determine if they would want to do the hike that you are recommending?

Hikers want to know:

Difficulty Level of Hike

A hiker needs to know if they can even perform the hike. If it is too technical or too physically challenging, many hikers may not be able to perform it. Include pictures that depict clearly how grueling the hike might be. This view of a challenging hike may intrigue some hikers to take your recommendation because they are up for the challenge. Alternatively, this might warn some hikers against this hike because it is too challenging for their current skill level. But it might spur them on to prepare for this hike at some later date, after they are more experienced.

Length of Hike

A hiker needs to know the length of the hike in both miles and hours or days. This will determine how much equipment is needed for the hike. If the hike you are recommending is a three-day hike, take pictures of all of the equipment that was packed for the trip. You can take pictures of the gear laid out beside the backpack to help them see all of the details. Then you can take other pictures of the gear all loaded up, so that you get a good frame of reference about how big the backpack is. Remember details are king here. Add those to a picture of a hiker, wearing the pack, standing on that trail where the view is great, and the pictures will have given the reader the key to what is in the story, instantly.

Amazing Scenes To Be Seen

One of the most compelling aspects of hiking is that you get to see places that you may not be able to get to any other way. Often, these places are seen by very few people and if they are incredibly unique and beautiful they are captured well by even fewer people. If you have captured amazing images with incredible or unique weather conditions or light conditions, it will be these images that will help you sell the story. People love beauty and they love the hope of being able to capture it as well as you did. Share just enough of the details about the hike to get the image that you shared, to give the reader a feel for the experience. Be sure to invite them to contact you for more details on the image.

Photography Magazine

For a photography magazine, the driver has to be amazing images. They must be different from the normal images that everyone else is capturing.

How do you get these unique images?

Don't look at everyone else's work for your inspiration. If you are traveling to some iconic place that millions of people go to, yes get the normal iconic images but then also start shooting your way. Spend time in a place and let the place inspire you. Pay attention to interesting light and interesting situations.

Go to places that no one else is going to.

Be out shooting at times when no one else is out capturing images.

Now that you have that amazing set of incredible images, you build the story of what inspired you to take them. Take people through your creative process. Everyone needs some inspiration, and you have no idea how you will inspire others. I must say, it is fun to see people copying your work.

Tell the story of the technical photographic details of the image. They will want to know what equipment you used to capture the image and what settings you had your camera set to, to make the image possible. People are hungry for this information.

Also, you will want to provide the details of the destination where you captured the image. They will need to know if it is accessible via car or hike or drone or any other method.

Traveling In Florence Italy

In this section, I am going to show you how to get three stories out of one four-day trip to Florence. You would have taken all of these pictures anyway, but with an idea of the separate stories ahead of time, you will be able to capture the perfect images for those stories, or you will be able to weave a story around any images you do get. Get these three ideas for stories into your mind: Iconic Locations, Hidden Gems, Best Food. Now let's focus on making sure we get all the best images for each story, or on creating a fantastic story to go with the images we do get.

Iconic Locations

Tell the story of these places from your readers perspective. Help them to feel the adventure, the passion, the emotion and know the history. Move them so they want to call their travel agent to book the trip. Everyone loves a great story, so use your images to tell the most iconic story possible.

For this type of story, your images must ideally be 'the best of the best' for these iconic places. You made sure you had a great list of all the top places and planned the time necessary at these places to photograph them in interesting light conditions with as few people as possible. You wanted to get interesting, high, and unique perspectives for your images where possible. But we all know that what we plan isn't always possible.

If, on the day that you visit, the weather was not helpful, or something else limited your ability to get the shots you wanted, then look at what you have – do you have some architectural detail shots, that you can weave a story around, about the construction of the place? What shots did you get, that you can create a unique story to support?

If you have a consistent style in your images, it will make your story that much more compelling.

Hidden Gems

This requires more research, but it can be an easier story to tell. As they are hidden, fewer people will know about them. Many people want to find and do that unique trip. These images do not need to be the best images of iconic places, but they still need to be very good and compelling. Again, you are looking to tug at people's emotions to move them to act.

The words that accompany your images for places like this need to focus around the elements of the place that your image captured – what stood out so much that you took that picture? What made that picture the essence of the location, so much so that you picked it out as one of your best shots? When you choose your best image from that location, it will tell you what story to tell – which of your notes are most appropriate, what extra research is needed to narrow down on what the image conveys.

Best Food In Florence

If you are a foodie, like I am, this one is just plain fun. It's guaranteed that you are going to eat in lots of places when travelling, and probably take pictures of almost every meal – so when you get back, you'll have lots of good food images. To craft a story around those becomes pretty straightforward, so long as you take a few notes as well as photos. (Pro tip – photograph the menu at the places you eat, as well as their streetfront or sign. This makes it far easier to write things up later.)

You can easily turn your normal eating habits into food stories too. List stories are always very hot, and this is a list anyone can do. This type of story could just as easily be about Best Chocolate, Best Gelato, or Best Wine. In this type of story, you are not claiming to be a professional food photographer, so your images do not need to be amazing (although it helps if they are). However, your images need to be very good and compel people to act. Here, using words that relate to the sense is critical – what did the food smell like? What did it taste like? What was the texture like? What did it sound like? (was the steak sizzling on the platter as it came out of the kitchen?) The image gives people what it looks like, the words provide that fully fleshed-out experience they can vicariously connect with.

Remember – this sort of story will be easier

to craft if, before your trip, you build your list of places you want to eat. While you are being seated try to get a seat near a window so that you have great natural light for your food images. Also, if possible try to set up your images so that you can see the food but also get a view of local attractions and ambiance. All of that aside, even with no careful prep, you'll almost certainly have some great food images – so don't waste them, write some stories!

Conclusion

If you plan your trips with the concepts demonstrated by these examples in mind, it will be easy to select the perfect images to pitch your stories to any editor, and to create the perfect stories to complement your best images – no matter what those images are of.

* * *

Wayne Moran is a Minnesota based travel photographer and artist, focused on landscapes, cityscapes, architectural, nature and portrait photography. His images are used commercially by book and magazine publishers, companies and organizations ranging from Financial Services firms, mom and pop ice cream shops and The Basilica of St Mary. Book, magazine and calendar publishers have featured his images in their publications and his photo-

graphs also grace the décor of many fine homes.
www.lettherebelightfineart.com

WRITING RULES: WHY THE BASICS MATTER

Anyone can become a travel writer. That is absolutely true. But it does require one critical thing: the ability to write. Learn, or reinforce some key basics, and your writing will shine.

By Kim Lambert

What exactly are the basics of good writing?

Let's look at a few of them.

Spelling

Remember, spelling is different depending on where you are in the world – British English and American English use different spellings, in many cases (for example, apologise is British, apologize is American) so check which version of English your target publication uses, and write accordingly. Spelling is also part of what makes the next point important.

Word Use

Use the right word. And make sure it is the right word. Don't just trust what you believe to be true. There are hundreds of examples in English of words that sound the same, but have different spellings and meanings (e.g. their, there and they're). There are also hundreds of examples of words that sound similar, are spelled differently, and have very different meanings, but are often confused (for example allusion, elision and illusion or allude and elude – do you know the distinct meanings of each of those words? If not, look them up!).

If you use the wrong word or the wrong spelling the end result could be an embarrassingly shifted meaning of your sentence. (e.g. if you say 'He alluded me' it actually has no meaning, but if you say 'He eluded me' it means that the person avoided you.) The dictionary online is your friend – use it.

Grammar

While you probably hated it at school, grammar matters, because getting this correct will remove ambiguity, making your writing clear. I will, however, qualify this one – 'correct' grammar will vary depending on where in the world you were taught and when in the last hundred years you were taught. Language shifts over time, and what is perceived as 'correct' shifts with it. So how do you deal with that, and still get it right?

As a first step, check the writers' guidelines of the publication you want to sell your article to – do they state what style guide they use? (e.g. Chicago Manual of Style) or do they have a downloadable document, explaining their preferences? Get that information, and write accordingly. Secondly, get someone to proofread your work – as many different people as you have available. They will each pick up different issues and over time you will learn which of your habits need changing.

A word of warning – do not trust Microsoft Word's grammar advice blindly – it is wrong about 25 percent of the time.

Tense

Tense is a subtle thing, surprisingly. There are gradations in the words we use in English, particularly with respect to past tense. Learn those subtleties, for clarity and conciseness. For example, people often say 'I wish I would have knew that' – which is horribly wrong! It should be 'I wish I had known that'. Examine your own language habits, and adjust where needed, because, if you don't get this right, the reader will struggle to know when you are writing about something that has already happened, compared to something happening now.

Writing Rules

When you write, there will always be people who look at your writing, and say 'Oh, that's wrong, you've broken this or that rule'. And sometimes those comments from two people will contradict each other. Don't panic; there is a reason for that. All of the things that we get taught at school, and at university, as 'writing rules' are not rules at all – they are guidelines, designed to allow people to write in a consistent and commonly understandable way. Most of them were introduced between 1850 and 1970, by various university professors who needed ways to get their students to be consistent, and (sometimes) who wanted to feel important by laying down the law. They are not absolute – in fact, part of developing your authentic personal writing voice is deciding which of those 'rules' you will choose to break, for effect.

So – treat these things as guidelines. Look at the rule, and ask 'why?' What does this rule help with? Why does it exist? Understanding the rules helps you to know when to use them.

Some things that have become rules in the last twenty years were nonexistent before – one of these is 'eliminate the word 'that' from your writing'. Let me say now – don't! Be judicious about it – sometimes the meaning is clear without 'that' in your sentence, sometimes it isn't. Leaving out 'that' can make it possible to read a sentence in multiple ways, rather than just the way you intended. Here is an example. If we write 'He made a point to remember Tom should be addressed as Sir Thomas when they were in public', it could confuse. It does so, because our mind absorbs the words in the order they arrive – so 'He made a point to remember Tom' is read as exactly that – a reminder to remember a person. But... that is not what the sentence is actually about. It should read 'He made a point to remember that Tom should be addressed as Sir Thomas when they were in public'. By having 'that' in the sentence, it tells the mind as you read, to look for qualifiers following the name, and allows the reader to recognize that it is not just about remembering the person's existence.

Flow

Anything you write should have a flow – when a person reads it they should not be conscious of the start and end of sentences or of the punctuation, because if you get things right it will seem so smooth and obvious that their mind will simply understand, and the content will be what they notice, not the structure delivering it. How do you create flow?

Vary your sentence lengths, so that it doesn't become repetitive or boring – too many short sentences in a row starts to feel like reading a dot point list, for example. Avoid 'run-on sentences' – if your sentence has the word 'and' in it more than once, it should probably be split into two smaller sentences.

Vary the length and complexity of the words you use, and don't repeat the same word too closely (eg, in the same sentence, or even paragraph) – find a synonym instead. Structure the ideas you are presenting into a logical pattern – does one thing depend on another? If so, you need to tell the reader about those things in the right order. In travel writing, you will generally want to lead into your article with some dramatic or rich scene-setting words (see the section below about engaging the senses) – background information or technical detail can come later.

The reader should feel pulled through your article, from start to finish, with no moments to pause going 'hey, what?' because something jars.

A Definition

'A travel writer's job is to make a place sound better, richer, and more fascinating than it actually is, so much so, that it motivates the reader to get up off the couch and book a trip to that place.'
(I have had this stated to me, by many people in the travel writing community – no one seems to know who first said it, but, whoever they were, they were wise indeed!)

Think about that definition for a moment. Then go and read some articles in a travel magazine – preferably about places you've actually been to. It's a very true definition. Now let's look at how you can do that with your writing, assuming you've got the basics we discussed above already working for you.

Engage All Of The Senses

When we stand in a real place, we notice it through every sense – sight, sound, smell, taste and touch. We see a building before us, which might be painted a very bright colour – we take that information in unconsciously – we might turn to whoever we are travelling with, and say 'hey, look at that building', but we don't need to say more, because they are there – they see the colour, they can walk up and touch the texture of the wall, they can smell the food smell from the café in its ground floor, they can hear the people talking in the café. But when we write, all the reader has is our words and whatever images the editor has chosen to go with the article.

Therefore, our words have to make up for all of the other senses.

We do that by writing about those senses and the feelings they evoke using words that are stronger and brighter than the words we would use in person.

'Look at that building', becomes 'three storeys of roughly rendered, bright blue painted building rose above the square, sheltering the café at its base, where chatting patrons lazed at tables set beneath red umbrellas, surrounded by the delicious scents of locally grown coffee and the traditional foods of the area.'

In that example, we have dealt with sight (color etc), smell (the scents of food and coffee), sound (the patrons chatting), taste (the food is delicious, because the scents are) and touch (the building is roughly rendered). We have also implied emotional aspects – if travel is about relaxation – our patrons are 'lazing' at the tables, having delicious food and drink – that immediately evokes in the reader the desire to be doing the same, or the memory of the last time they did that.

Go For The Emotions

People travel for the experience of places that are different from home, for the chance to feel different. Your writing should evoke feelings – no matter what it's about. Depending on the place, person or event you are writing about, you may wish to evoke happiness, sadness, the sense of freedom, joy – in fact, almost any emotion we can experience. That could even be anger - if the article is for a magazine focused on social justice in poorer countries, you may be aiming to get the reader angry about the inequities that exist.

When a reader feels an emotion as they read your article, they are far more likely to act after reading it – to click the link at the end, to book the holiday, to donate to the cause. And that's exactly the result you want.

Make It Compact

You only get so many words and you need to make them count. So, write your first draft, count the words, then go back through it and ask yourself: 'What words can I take out, without changing the meaning, and without losing the impact?'

Take out those words and check your word

count again. Then go through and ask yourself: 'Are there any places where I have used two words that could be replaced by one word with the same meaning?' (e.g. you might have said 'wooden chair' but does what it is made of matter? Could you just use 'chair'?)

Change any that you can. Then go through and make sure your senses and emotion-evoking words are as impactful as possible, and there are as few of them as possible to describe any one thing. How much you'll need to fiddle here will depend on how tight your word count target is.

In summary: make your writing as impactful as possible in as few words as possible. Hook the reader, reel them in, and keep them reading to the end in one smooth emotional experience.

Key Point

Get the basics right – spelling, grammar, word usage, tense and flow – and you will find it far easier to then polish your writing for emotional impact – and your editor will love you, because they have less work to do!

* * *

Kim Lambert is a speaker, photographer, writing and publishing Coach, a travel writer and a multi-time Amazon bestselling author, with more than

70 books published to date. She is also the owner of a publishing company, Dreamstone Publishing, which publishes books for a variety of authors, and also works with other large publishing companies to enhance and update their current catalogues for digital book delivery.

FEES, FINANCES AND THE BUSINESS OF TRAVEL WRITING

FOREWORD BY RACHAEL ROWE

People dream of becoming a travel writer and many reach their goal. Most of us want to sit under a palm tree beside a beach with a laptop producing stories for various media platforms. But sometimes things don't work out that way. There's a massive reality check when bills arrive and the practicalities of making a living sink in. How do you live the dream but keep a handle on reality?

This section has some practical and valuable advice from experienced travel writers who have let readers in on some of the ways they work to make a decent living from writing. One issue any freelancer will eventually run into is the pain of unpaid invoices. Washington (DC)-based travel writer Andrew Madigan suggests some effective methods that might persuade those 'forgetful' editors to pay up – as long as they're used with professional tact and a good dash of humor. As he notes: "Sometimes it's perfect. A new gig. Good money. The editor is easy to work with. She loves your writing and doesn't want to change a word .... Nothing could be better."

But before you get to that idyllic state, many writers have to start out by juggling two careers while transitioning into a full-time writer. That can make it tough to find the time to write as well as the time to travel. MaryRose Denton articulates in her chapter how this worked for her, giving lessons to use in everyday practice. She offers simple steps that anyone can take on a daily basis - a tried and tested way of making a dream achievable.

When life gets in the way of traveling, finding inspiration and paying work can be difficult. A novice travel writer does not have the access to press trips and sponsorship that someone more established may have. Life events happen, meaning you have to rethink how you work. So what do you do? Lucy Bryson has been in that position and has written an insightful chapter that is solution focused. Many of her tips and experiences are useful for any writer looking to specialise in travel.

Keeping the income streams flowing is an essential skill for any travel writer. It is crucial to stay ahead of the trends and look for opportunities that will pay. Income can come from unexpected sources as writer Christa Bedwin reveals in her chapter. Sharing knowledge, and developing niche areas are just two of the ways to find a profitable way of writing. Networking and promoting your business positively are crucial.

The writers in this section advocate promoting a business like stance to work and valuing yourself as a writer. This helps you find profitable work and keep your business healthy.

❊ ❊ ❊

Rachael Rowe is a travel and health writer from Dorset, England. She has authored walking guides and guidebooks and writes for online and print publications.

WHAT TO DO WHEN THE EDITOR DOESN'T PAY

What to do when you're not paid and what your legal rights are. How tricky this becomes when dealing with overseas publications. How to manage all this with tact and profes-sionalism. And humour.

By Andrew Madigan

L oud cursing, at first. Pounding the key-board. Jim Beam in a rocks glass. None of this helps, really: You need Plan B.

Freelancing isn't easy. You have to track down

editors, pitch your stories, and hope they respond. If they do, you just might land an assignment. You also hope to be paid – in real money, that is, not in contributor copies or 'getting your work out ther'. You can't pay the phone bill in 'getting your work out there's'.

So you have an assignment. Great. You write the piece, revise and edit, send it to the editor.

Maybe you're asked for a few cuts or changes. Maybe the publisher has a query or two. But now your job's done, right? Time to sit back and relax.

Not always.

Editors have left me in the lurch about 20 times. In fact, I've become expert in not getting paid.

That's awesome, I know. On the plus side, it's happened so many time I know what to do about it.

The First Step

You always remember the first time. A small fiction magazine owed me $25. What could I do?

After several emails to the editor, all unanswered, I went to Facebook with my troubles. A number of writers responded to my post with their own tales of slippery editors and flimflam journals. I was looking for advice but didn't find anything concrete or practical.

I wrote to the Chamber of Commerce in the town where the magazine was published, but no one wrote back. Thanks a lot, local civic organization.

In a fit of desperation, I started a Facebook group called I Hate _____ [the magazine name].

This received hundreds of Likes. Word got around to the editor, who, in garbled legalese borrowed from Law & Order, demanded that I "seize and desist." He said I'd already been paid, posting a picture of a check with my name on it. I replied this was proof that a check had been cut, not that it had been mailed to me or that I'd cashed it. "Show me the canceled check!" I demanded. This triggered another flood of 'Likes'. I never heard from the guy again. He seized and desisted.

Afterward, I started wondering why he had a photo of my check. Pretty strange.

I never got the $25.

Despite my long fruitless journey, I was on to something. The Chamber of Commerce was a good idea.

Have Bigger Friends

A few months later I was stiffed by a prestigious

food magazine. "We can't pay much," were the first words out of the editor's mouth, which was an understatement. She didn't pay me anything at all.

This time I tried the Better Business Bureau, which is the loud and assertive older brother of the Chamber of Commerce. The one who stands in front of the mirror looking at his biceps all day and is pretty useful in a fight. I submitted a formal complaint and my comments were forwarded to the magazine. A few days later the editor responded with a breezy assurance that my check was in the mail. "So sorry," she said. "Just slipped my mind." Right. She just forgot to pay me for 18 months, and forgot to open any of my follow-up emails. Sounds reasonable. I was paid two days later.

My next scrap was with a well-respected liquor magazine. I submitted the copy – a profile of a local distillery – well before deadline. The article was slated for the following month.

Six months elapsed. Eight. Ten. I was asked for rewrites. My article was too long. No problem, I lopped off 25%.

Four more months went by. Six. Eight. The editor asked me to add a few details. He gave me a list of new topics to address. I revised the article, again. It was now twice as long as the editor had originally commissioned, but naturally I wasn't paid double the rate.

In fact, I wasn't paid at all. Six months after submitting the final copy, I asked when the article would be coming out. "See if you can get some more photos," the editor said. "I don't like what the distiller sent me." Well, long story short, the distiller couldn't send new photos. I forwarded this news to the editor, who didn't respond.

Another eight months elapsed. I emailed the editor. No reply. I emailed again, the next month.

No reply. I searched through the magazine website until I found an email address for the publisher, who puts out a half-dozen liquor magazines. He said he'd look into it.

Meanwhile, I sought the help of Small Claims Court. He's the badass cousin of the Better Business Bureau, who did time in juvey and has a skull tattoo on his forehead. The SCC – there's one in every state – is perfect for settling minor labor disputes. You don't need a lawyer. The trial is quick and easy. In this case, we had a contract: Money for services rendered. I'd done the work, but I hadn't been paid. It was a simple matter. You can file for up to $5,000 in compensation, so I asked for the missing payment plus expenses for traveling to the court date and work hours lost while dealing with this issue. A $500 gig that would pay out $2,500.

The next day I got an email from the editor: "We're not running the piece. The photos were no good. You won't get paid."

I replied, cc'ing the publisher. The problem, I explained, was that the editor hadn't examined the photos until more than a year after they'd been sent to him – by the subject of the profile, not me. I had nothing to do with it. Had the editor done his job in a timely manner, he would've had better photos. I further explained – politely, firmly, reasonably – that he'd done very little during our work together except avoid emails, ignore the established timetable, change his expectations, and make excuses. He'd demonstrated a pattern of avoidance and fraud by withholding payment and ducking my emails. I attached a copy of my Small Claims complaint and made it clear that I would take them to court if I wasn't paid.

The publisher sent me a letter, fulsome with apologies. He offered me $1,500 if I didn't take them to court. I said I only wanted what was fair, $500. Three days later, I got the check.

Small Claims is a great service for the little guy. You can get justice, and your back pay, without waiting long or hiring an attorney. There are other state and local agencies that can help you out, too, such as the Department of Labor. Getting in touch with your local congressperson is also an option.

Phone Dead-end?

You may be wondering if I ever pick up the phone to call one of these miscreant editors. No I did not. For starters, I rarely pick up the phone to call anyone. I do almost all my work remotely, by email. I only speak to editors on the phone once every few years, and I meet them in person even less often than that.

What's more, the newspapers and magazines I write for rarely supply phone numbers for their staff, especially the editors. They don't want to be bothered by pesky writers like me, who want to know why their wonderful article was hacked apart with an editing pen, or, even worse, not accepted for publication. If there is a number listed on the website, it's almost always answered by an assistant, who would be unlikely to put me through to an editor, or voice mail. In either case I'd have to leave a message, and, if I ever got an answer, it would probably be through email.

So sure, I could've tried getting an editor on the phone, but it would have taken longer and, in all likelihood, been a dead-end.

Research First

What happens if the editor is based in another country? Recouping your fee can a tricky process. What I recommend is this: do your research first. Is it a reputable publication? Does the editor have a LinkedIn account? What does the internet say about his or her business practices? If a web search of "publication name + scam" yields a few angry hits, consider yourself warned.

A few years ago I was approached by an editor based in Qatar. She was professional and polished, the magazine looked legit, and Google didn't have anything nasty to say. I accepted the work. However, I asked for half the money up front, and explained—in polite and apologetic language—that if she never paid me it would be exceedingly difficult to recover the payment. The editor was understanding and agreed to the deal. I wrote the piece, received full payment, and they commissioned a number of future assignments from me.

I could go on ad almost literally nauseum. There are many species of disreputable editors: the ones who commission a piece but don't follow up with concrete details and are never heard from again; the ones who kill your article without letting you know and then block your emails; the ones who send you to some Accounts Payable drone who claims that an internal audit is "holding things up," or asks you to submit an invoice for the third time, or says that a computer glitch will "take just a few months to fix."

Life can be a challenging for a freelancer. Chasing work, tracking down payment, wrestling with unscrupulous editors.

But then sometimes it's perfect. A new gig. Good money. The editor is easy to work with. She loves your writing and doesn't want to change a word. She immediately offers you new assignments. You get up in the morning, put on a fresh pot of coffee. You work in the comfort of your own home, which means you don't have to get dressed or fight through traffic. There's no fussy boss lurking in the next room. This is why you got into the business in the first place.

Nothing could be better.

❊ ❊ ❊

Andrew Madigan is a freelance writer and novelist based in Washington, DC. His first novel Khawla's Wall, is published by Second Wind, and his second book, Altar Boys, is coming out soon. He's lived and worked in Tokyo, Okinawa, Korea, Abu Dhabi, Dubai, the UK, and all over the US.

8 WAYS TO EARN MONEY AS A WRITER, BEYOND MAGAZINES

Knowing and taking advantage of multiple ways to find profitable work is vital for travel writers.

by Christa Bedwin

This article is a jumble of the many tips and ways that I have found good work – some that you probably haven't thought of yet, and some of the usual ways. If you have questions, I'm happy to correspond through social media. Come find me!

I grew up hearing that writing wasn't a real job, so I went to university for a B.Sc. and a B.Ed. and squashed all my novelist dreams. But the laugh's on them. Looking back, I realize that the majority of my income has been from writing and editing, anyway.

Meanwhile, I have travelled to more than 40 countries, raised one good strong mannerly son, and in some years, earned six figures as a writer and editor. Most other years, I prefer earning less and having more fun. But it's possible, if you want, to earn great money as a writer.

While I have earned excellent money from a few magazine articles, I have found that most magazine work requires so much marketing, e-mailing and begging that it ends up being a lot of hours for the pay you get. Of course, magazines are fun and still worth doing, but there are easier ways to make money as a writer, ones where the clients will come to you instead of you chasing them down every time.

Here are some lucrative tips to find the types of jobs that have turned writing into my main earning activity over the past twenty years.

1. Help Other People Share Their Knowledge

Experts need to report on their findings. While they may be high-level experts in their field with a high degree of technical knowledge, they often are also smart enough to know that they need help with the writing so others can understand their message. In addition, they often have the money to hire professional writers, either through their own salaries or through grants.

These contracts are not just lucrative, they can also be inspiring. I loved helping a community-minded guy self-publish his financial advice book. I loved helping some farmers write up their knowledge on a new-but-old sustainable crop to spread the knowledge through his farming community. I love following along with my clients' research year-to-year.

Training: Make yourself a specialist in translating technical jargon to plain language. There are many high-quality professional webinars available online through Editors Canada and other associations.

How to get this type of work: Be visible in your community. Give lectures in your organization (step one: Belong to organizations, whether it's the Society for Technical Communications, an Editors' association, or a quality writers' association). Speak up on your professional association email lists or Facebook pages with useful, intelligent information (e.g. I'm a chemistry specialist, and I've always offered help on chemistry questions, so people know I'm a go-to person for chemistry, though I also chat about other editing issues.) Then, people come to you when they need your specific type of writing and editing.

Some personal examples:

The financial book's author found my name, along with other editors, on our local editors' association website. He interviewed us all and liked my handshake best and hired me.

The farmers knew me in the community through me offering help that was unrelated to editing, but we got to conversation while volunteering. Just go out and be useful and friendly in any context that you enjoy.

Researchers often similarly find me by word of mouth, because other writers and editors who know I edit science texts pass on my name. Get to be useful to, and friendly with, such colleagues.

2. Specialize In Research

University and industry researchers must write to keep their positions. They write academic articles and grant proposals and loads of email communications. Another common feature of academics is that they travel – meaning that there are many, many English-Second-Language researchers who understand the value of hiring an English expert to help them revise their research papers and grant proposals and even emails, to put their best foot forward. I love working with them because they're brilliant and often so grateful.

Hot tip on this one: have a university or college specialty besides English, and target university departments with your specialty, whether it's physics or psychology. No need to keep this local – ask any and every place where people work with your specialty. Chances are very high that they will have English-Second-Language researchers who need help with grants and articles, and who have budgets to do so. University work is all about publishing, and articles need to be polished to get into reputable journals.

Training: Find academic editors' associations on Facebook or other places on the web. If you got a university degree, chances are that you already know many of the things that qualify you for this work (referencing, citing sources, credible research, and so on)

3. Help People Share Community Information

While putting together community newsletters might not earn you very much money, you can learn valuable writing, formatting, and publishing techniques and processes through helping with a community newsletter, and later extend that to, for example, alumni magazines, which are often well-funded. Showing excellence in the community can also help to build your portfolio. Your name will appear in the issues online.

It's another way to network and meet people. Other types of work will follow through word of mouth, as long as you keep speaking up about what you are able to do and building a portfolio of excellent work and excellent relationships. (Caveat: Part of creating excellent relationships is choosing to leave ones that are not great, which you will also encounter. Do not stay over-long in any position, volunteer or paid, that does not feel like it's lifting you up.)

4. Be Businesslike

Attend entrepreneur and business networking opportunities in your neighbourhood or online. Personally, these have not yielded me too many profitable writing opportunities, but they help me stay in a businesslike state of mind, help me meet more people, and inspire me with ideas.

The main lesson is: keep your eyes and mind open. You never know who might know someone who knows someone else who is wanting to self-publish a book and needs a hand. And busy, social people who are interested in business cost-benefit analyses may be people who realize that they would rather pay you to write for them, than take the time and energy to do it themselves. Don't expect everyone to understand that trade off, but do develop your radar for who the successful people are who will value you, and spend money on you.

5. Get Skills That People Need And Don't Have

Learn formatting to help people self-publish on Amazon. Learn website building to help people get their message out on the web. People will hire you because you can do something they can't, you can do something better than they can do, or you can do something that they don't have time for. The pay scale is sliding – the more you can do that they can't do, the more highly they'll value you.

6. Get Linked In With Linkedin

One place to showcase your writing and your specialties is on the LinkedIn career platform. I have about 200 articles up there, starting with grammar advice for engineers and ranging over any topic that moved me – lots of yoga lessons aimed to certain issues (like desk workers in chairs, anxiety, dealing with stress), some travel reflections, some grant-writing advice... in a way, what you write doesn't matter as much as how you write it. Write it well, so that it show-cases what you can do.

I got hired on a $10,000 English exam-writing contract because the project manager said "Well, it's clear that you can write," even though high school English was not my area of expertise. LinkedIn also lets me send friendly hellos to my contacts periodically, who might need me at a future date. (Note: I mean specific notes to individuals such as: "How did your mother's surgery go?" or "Did your son get that scholarship he was hoping for?" These are relationship-building genuine hellos, not mass spam emails, which likely lose more connections than they gain.)

7. Textbooks, Textbooks, And Textbooks

There is an endless market for new textbooks, so they are constantly in production and need writers, editors, copyeditors, designers, proofreaders, answer checkers... chances are if you're a great writer, you also have the skills to do some of this. State/province/regional authorities love to monkey around with the curriculum, and every time they change it, a whole new wave of textbook writing is triggered. If you can write, it is not difficult to learn how to write standardized exam questions, good study guides, and so on.

How to get this type of work

Once you get a little bit of experience showing that you are a hard worker and smart writer for educational materials, word of mouth will have you rolling in as much work as you're willing to take on. For decades. At least, that's what happened to me!

8. Speaking Of Word Of Mouth....

Your contacts are precious. I got years of work through someone who I had beer with at an editors' conference. Find those conferences and associations. Volunteer with them early in your career (or any time really) to make connections, and cultivate your connections – tend them like a precious garden plant by offering them value – answers in conversations, praise and encouragement on their Facebook pages, friendly meaningful hellos in their messenger periodically – these niceties that some people think are just "old fashioned" manners are actually how people with a lot of money decide where they spend it – on high quality people. Act and deliver in ways that make you a high-quality person, and people will pass your name around.

It's the same with your academic writing and editing clients – when they're happy with you, they'll share your name with friends. I have clients who have used me for their papers and grants for more than a decade now. When you build up a list of clients like that, you don't need to advertise much.

And... what probably doesn't work:

Many freelancers start out thinking that the mass-appeal freelance job websites are going to magically yield a lot of clients and earn them a living. However, sites like these are an impersonal race to the bottom price where you may have trouble getting people to value you at what you're worth. I do know one editor who has built up quality relationships and a few clients who pay her reasonably through a site like that, but it took her a long time. My own experience, and those of others I know, is that these large clearing-house writing opportunities often end up with your clients disappearing, or paying you only a pittance. Which leads me to my last point...

Aim High: An Essential Note About Your Value!

Do not waste much energy trying to convince community members, neighbours, or family members that you are worth $20 or $40 or $80 or $120 per hour. Whatever your rate is, some people will never pay it. Others will pay it with joy and gratitude!

Don't try to get restaurant owners to pay you to fix their menus... most don't feel that they have the money for that, or that it's worth it to them. Do look for people who are reaching higher in their own careers, and need excellent writing to do it.

Focus on finding the people who will pay you money for the quality of your writing. Once you start building up a portfolio in paying directions, you can command higher and higher rates, because your expertise and experience will help others portray what they need to, and help them make money.

Remember: People will hire you because

- you can do something they can't,
- you can do something better than they can
- you can do something that they don't have time for

If you are a talented writer, there are a lot of people who need you – and some of these people will pay for your words. The way to be visible to those people is to make yourself heard. Join associations. Speak up. Offer assistance in ways that showcase your own excellence to people who will value you and understand the value of good communication. Do not waste energy trying to convince people who do not value you. These principles are the same whether your relationships with people are in-person or online, but hopefully you can establish relationships, and find work, in both spheres. Work for people who love what you do, and you'll love your work!

❋ ❋ ❋

Christa Bedwin has been an international science editor and writer for 20 years. She has travelled to 45 countries (living in several along the way), written three writing textbooks for consultants, and contributed chapters to Editing Canadian English, as well as various freelance writing experiences with magazines, educational and trade publishers, industry, government, and scientific writers around the globe. As time and money allow, she is now chipping away at her real "when I grow up" dream job -- writing time travel romantic adventure novels inspired by her travels.

HOW TO MAKE A LIVING AS A TRAVEL WRITER WHEN LIFE GETS IN THE WAY

Being grounded in one place doesn't have to mean changing the course of your career.

By Lucy Bryson

B ack in 2010, I was tramping across the high, cold mountains of Northern Argentina and Bolivia, thumbing for lifts in rural Paraguay, grabbing sleep on bumpy over-night buses and trying to avoid electric shocks on the rare occasions I found lodgings with a hot shower. I was on assignment for the Rough Guide to South America on a Budget, and, being footloose and child-free, thought nothing of renting out my one-bedroom apartment in Rio de Janeiro while I set off hauling my backpack around the Andes. A few months later, the dis-covery that my partner and I were expecting brought much excitement, but also signaled the end - at least for a while - of such devil-may-care travel adventures.

Fast forward to 2019, and I have an eight-year-old daughter in full time education at a Portu-guese school. As a single mother with no family easily at hand (a direct result of spending most of my adult life living thousands of miles away from my home city of Manchester, UK), I can't just pitch up and go globe-trotting whenever work calls for it.

But I still have to pay the bills, and, having carved out a career of sorts in the field of travel writing, it's still my preferred way to feed my fast-growing daughter and keep a roof over our heads.

As any travel writer knows, this profession is unlikely to make you rich. And for freelancers, that's a truth that becomes more obvious with each passing year, as the in-boxes fill up with offers to assign work at wincingly low rates or, worse still, for no payment other than the dreaded 'exposure'.

And sometimes life just gets in the way of travel - whether it's family commitments, a 'day job' or anything else that keeps you tied to one place for a while - when you can't jump on a plane at the drop of a hat, how can you actually land the assignments that you hope will actually pay the bills?

Here are a few things that have worked for me:

Write What You Know

Write about what and where you know (and apologies if that sounds obvious). Most travel writers will have picked up on the increasing demand for content written by 'local experts. While living in Rio de Janeiro, Brazil, I regularly wrote one-off 'insider pieces' on request, as well as being the go-to Rio writer for Fodor's Travel, and the Rio local expert for USA Today 10Best and the now-defunct Planet Eye. It wasn't mega-bucks but it was regular work that kept the wolf from the door, paying a few hundred dollars a month each.

When I moved to Portugal in 2015, living by the beach just outside Lisbon, I made sure I quickly became familiar enough with the local scene that I could transfer my writing attentions to the city (I quickly landed assignments with Fodor's, Vice Munchies and Gastro Obscura,as well as writing occasional 'hot new opening' tidbits for TimeOut and blog posts for Urban Travel Guide) while keeping an eye on Rio - I still regularly write about that lovely, troubled city, having used my local knowledge of Brazil recently to land stories with BBC Travel, Atlas Obscura, and others. It's worth looking out for print and online publications that have a 'local expert' and checking to see if there is a vacancy in your city. Even if the pay isn't terrific, it might help pave the way for better paying articles.

Have Some Anchor Clients

It's good to have some solid clients that know and appreciate your work, and will keep coming back to you when they want coverage in your area of expertise. For example, I've been writing and updating guidebook chapters for Fodor's for over 10 years, and various Fodor's editors have approached me for everything from one-off website articles to batches of hotel reviews - payment ranges from $200-ish for articles to several thousand dollars for updating or writing guidebook chapters (but be aware there is a LOT of fact-checking and hard work as well as the 'fun part' of visiting hotels, restaurants etc.

Pitching can be a lonely process - all those ideas sent into the ether, the replies of 'we'll pass' or, worse - crickets - but sending out regular pitches to high profile outlets can pay dividends - for example, one BBC or Atlas Obscura story might pay $400-600, whereas your 'anchor client' may pay less, but with more regular work. I probably get around 30-40 per cent of my work based on pitches I have sent out, and the remainder from clients I have worked with in the past and who contact me when they need something.

Travel Locally

Being a travel writer doesn't have to mean flying half way across the world - you can use weekends from your day job or school responsibilities to get on a bus across town to see some cool new street art, visit a restaurant you've heard locals getting excited about, take in a kooky arts event or festival. Wherever you live, and however mundane the activity seems to you, there's sure to be something of interest from an outsider perspective. Sell your local status and connections to the community as your strength, and try to make yourself the obvious choice for any editor looking to commission content about your region.

Spending my summers in Manchester, I have a whole lot of local knowledge about that rainy-but-lovely city, too, and have been assigned Manchester articles by Fodor's and TimeOut. I try to make it my business (quite literally) to be up to speed with the cultural goings on in all the places I call (or have called) home. I look out for local cultural curiosities: from 'poop liqueur' to hidden Chinese restaurants via mega-clown gatherings...and get pitching these local insights.

See Holidays As Work Opportunities

As I'm pretty much limited to traveling outside term time, I try to use quick breaks as opportunities to land work assignments. Curious to visit the Azores, for example, I used a school break for Carnival to visit the island, and the (inexpensive) trip paid for itself when I landed an article writing about the island's happy cows for Vice Munchies. A trip to Northern Portugal was an opportunity to land assignments writing about the Minho Wine Region and Portugal's only National Park, but I also discovered that the north's 'penis cakes' were a big hit with editors. I'm currently in Porto during the first week of my daughter's school holidays, combining sightseeing with updating a Porto guidebook chapter for Fodor's.

Scour the web

Pitching is a necessary evil for freelancers, but we can try to ease some of the soul-sapping sensation of pitching into the void by keeping an eagle eye out for calls for stories that fit your niche.. If you're reading this, chances are that you're familiar with PitchWhizz, the website that streamlines the pitching process for writers and editors, while TravMedia also features regular calls for pitches, while Sian Meades' Freelance Writing Jobs newsletter is a carefully curated list of openings for freelancers and remote work as well as more permanent positions. There are several Facebook groups out there - several of which are secret groups, so you might need to work those journo connections to get an invite.

Be prepared to go to the 'dark side' sometimes

Nobody's suggesting you actually sell your soul, but sometimes the siren call of PR writing, copy writing and other non-journo assignments is going to prove too strong to resist, especially if you have bills to pay and mouths to feed, as rates tend to be higher than for other types of writing work. There's no shame in having a 'side hustle', even if it doesn't fill your soul with joy.

❊ ❊ ❊

Lucy Bryson is a freelance travel writer from Manchester, UK. She has lived with her daughter in a seaside town just outside Lisbon, Portugal, since 2015, and previously lived in Rio de Janeiro, Brazil, for close to 10 years. She has been published in BBCTravel, Atlas Obscura, TimeOut, Vice, Rough Guides, Culture Trip, Matador Network, Footprint,

USA Today and Fodor's, among others.

BRIDGING CAREERS: MANAGING THE DAY-JOB-TO-DREAM TRANSITION

"A journey of a thousand miles must begin with a single step." *Lao Tzu's famous saying rings especially true for those beginning a new job or career change. Any task, however long, begins with making that initial step, the first action towards an end goal.*

By Mary Rose Denton

When I began my freelance writing career I was still holding down a full-time job. The challenge was bridging the two careers and finding balance along the way. "How do I phase out of one career while building the other?" This was just one of the many questions that surfaced over and over again. Here are some of the challenges I faced while building a writing career, and ways to manage them.

Take the First Step

I had a dream, and I am willing to bet you do too. My dream was to become a full-time freelance writer. Many people talk about wishing to write but don't know where to begin. Sometimes this is out of fear, perhaps of the unknown, sometimes it is from procrastination, self-doubt, or a lack of knowing where to start. The secret is simple yet challenging. Just start, one step in front of the other. J.P. Morgan said, "The first step to getting somewhere is to decide you are not going to stay where you are."

A few years back, I made that decision, to take that first step. I was at the proverbial crossroads of life. Newly divorced, approaching a milestone birthday, and questioning where I wanted life to take me next, I decided to set out on this path to pursue my writing goals. The decision to move forward made, I felt a new thirst and vigor to learn this craft. The next question was "How do I begin?"

Learn the Craft

During those first baby steps I immersed myself in anything and everything I could find to read regarding a career in freelance writing. I trawled the internet soaking up article after article and blog after blog. I found a niche in travel writing and decided to begin there by enrolling in an online course not only to learn the step-by-step ropes but also to find a network of other writers doing the same thing.

What I discovered became invaluable. The course itself outlined processes of pitching ideas, crafting articles, finding publications and building a career. But the real value came as I found myself surrounded by like-minded people working and doing the same thing I was aiming to achieve.

However, while I was reading about the best ways to pitch a story and follow up with editors, there were still bills to pay and groceries to buy. Everyday life continued as I learned the skills needed to become a full time writer. As a single mom, I did not have a cushion or a second income to bridge me over those humps. There were days the balancing act seemed far more precarious than solidly balanced. That is just life, and unfortunately where some people may give up.

Networking

What helped see me through the slumps and frustrations was surrounding myself with a network of other writers. An important "take action" step is to reach out for support and connect with others in your community. I became a member of several writing organizations, which I could also add to my resume, as well as local groups and writing chapters. My first connections were made through my online course then through attending a local writer's conference, and eventually connecting with other writers and editors in local chapter groups.

Even with limited amounts of time, I reached out and grew this portion of my career slowly but steadily, one connection and one step at a time. The most important thing was to just get out there, meet people who will offer support and I can support in turn. Each step like this strengthened my resolve to keep going and take another step forward.

Do Something Everyday

Probably the most important thing in finding balance and avoiding the common feeling of being overwhelmed is to take small steps. Doing something each day moved me in the direction of my goals. I already knew this from running my own business, but I still wanted to rush into this new travel writing world with excitement and exuberance!

Taking small steps allowed me to apply skills I already had from running a successful small business, such as showing up and being present. I quickly realized I needed to treat writing as a job, and not a hobby - as much as my day job that paid the bills. This required carving out time to write or work on the business of writing. I needed to make writing the priority. The laundry could wait, the dishes, and to-do lists too. It required focus and hard work to be successful. Even the small things each day are drops in the bucket for your goals. They add up.

On days where words and writing inspirations failed, perhaps perusing some new periodicals pushed me forward as I looked over their writing content. Reviewing a magazine's writing guidelines can get ideas churning as to what fits their niche. I then added these to my spreadsheet of publications to pitch. Creating a new pitch and hitting that "send" button always seemed to regenerate my creativity. Some days I only had time for a few minutes spent on social media connecting with others in the writing world or a quick email sent to an editor. But it was something. Each day I actively worked on some aspect of my writing career, even if it was only for a few snippets of moments.

Be Patient With Yourself

Patience is a virtue. Be patient with yourself and the process. Each day, often many times a day, I would have a chat with myself as a reminder that each step would keep me moving forward. It is all too easy to become overwhelmed, especially with social media at our fingertips. With the click of a button or a swipe of our finger we can get lost in the abundance of information on the web. We read what other writers are doing and compare ourselves to it. That is part of human nature. When impatience sets in, take a step back, make a list of all your accomplishments, take stock, in order to see the path you are on and the road ahead of you.

Spending time in nature can expand our minds as well as ground us in the here and now. Take a walk, bike, hike, work in the garden or lie in the sand listening to crashing waves. I found time in nature to be ritualistic or prepared myself to write with a yoga meditation. Exercising my body helped me focus my mind which in turn led to productivity and another small step towards my goals.

Bridging careers - beginning a writing career while holding down a full-time job - can be tricky. There is no blueprint or starters manual, for each person's path to their goals will look entirely different, cultivated by our own unique situations, life circumstances, and dreams. But it is imperative to keep putting one foot in front of the other, to take a breath and acknowledge your own accomplishments, and to always move forward.

*   *   *

MaryRose Denton is a freelance writer, traveler, licensed massage therapist, lifelong vegetarian, and most importantly a mother. She enjoys the mash up of these that life brings and writes about them with insight, humor, and wit. She is a member of ITWPA, IFWTWA, IAPWE, TravMedia, Travel Massive WA, Media Kitty.

RELATION-SHIPS, NETWORKING AND CLIENT MANAGEMENT

FOREWORD BY FFION LLWD-JONES

Just as with most worthwhile things, building a business network is a long-term strategy that yields freelance success – and the good news is: You can start doing it today.

Hang on, though!

That's easy to say, but does it sometimes seem there's already so much pressure to do so much ... not just getting the gigs, but also researching, writing, proofing, editing, following up, invoicing ... and on and on ... and now you need to create space for serious networking, too?

But here's the good (maybe great) thing: the network you build will actually give you much more than it takes. In time, it will lead to better-paid travel gigs, unusual destination opportunities, and position you as an in-demand freelance travel writer.

And, because you have this book, you won't be alone on that building path: five experts have generously shared their suggestions and tips on everything travel 'networking' - from the initial approach, to leveraging those budding relationships, making friends with PR people – and even how to collect on the occasional unpaid invoices (your network will be yielding so much work, there's bound to be a few of those).

So, to help you get started, travel writer Chez Chesak is your personal guide to leveraging personal networks, travel shows and travel associations to get the stories you want and the editors you need. Whether you're new to travel writing, or an experienced senior professional, Chez's key networking suggestions are investments into building the writing career that you want. As he comments: "After all, everyone you meet has the possibility to open a door for you, someday."

And, once you've got your basic network in place (and are still building it), remember to make it sustainable. Content writer, editor and consultant Jo Ostgarden comments: "New writers, in particular, need to consider sustainability. Keeping work flowing and payments rolling is the only way this life works if you want to make a living at it."

In this chapter, Jo shares her knowledge and suggestions for sharing work and bringing sustainability to your work as the opportunity arises.

And still looking to the future (remember the long-term strategy?) freelance writer and author (Disney Demystified: The Stories and Secrets Behind Disney's Favorite Theme Park Attractions) David Mumpower shares his secrets of leveraging now for the future. He says: "Improve yourself as a professional and as a person by demonstrating kindness and saying yes more often. You'll discover myriad benefits of this behavior that will bleed into all parts of your life."

And in another string to your growing network, forming relationships with public relations (PR) people can be wonderful, if it's approached professionally. As Australian-based freelance food, travel and lifestyle writer Lindy Alexander says: "Quite simply, PRs are some of the most important people you need to connect with (and stay connected with) if you want to be a successful travel writer."

In her chapter, Lindy covers all the steps to that success, from how to get invited on your first 'fam' trip, working on the road, and - perhaps most important of all - keeping in touch with your PR network.

Despite being in this business for more than 20 years, I'm still learning. And I was as excited to read these chapters as you probably are - or certainly should be! The generously shared experience and advice can save you time, and create wonderful new opportunities, all because you're taking those first steps on the networking path. Have fun!

❋ ❋ ❋

Ffion Llwyd-Jones is a Welsh-born writer and editor who makes words work! Her stories are in magazines (digital and print) across the world, including North America, Australia, Europe and the UK. And the results of her editor's 'red pen' are reflected in many high-quality newsletters, periodicals, magazines, case studies and features. She is - of course - currently writing a novel about magic, time travel and a silver amulet:)

NETWORKING YOUR WAY TO THE TOP

Leverage personal networks, travel shows and travel associations to get the stories you want and the editors you need.

By Chez Chesak

Perhaps you're new to travel writing. You're young, changing careers, or suddenly find yourself in travel. You don't know anyone – or maybe anything – yet. Just as a journey of a thousand miles begins with a single step, you can only start with the beginning and by taking one step at a time.

So how do you create a network of editors, colleagues and (perhaps) admirers to help elevate your travel writing career? Some of my suggestions may be costly in both time and money, especially if you're just starting out. But if you're serious about expanding your network and promoting yourself to editors, media relations people, other writers and many of the other industry professionals who make the industry move, these are key networking opportunities that have worked for me over the years, and that I would recommend even if you don't do them all the time, or all at the same time. They are investments into building the writing career that you want.

Start Close to Home

First, get to know other travel writers as well as any friends of friends or family in the travel space. Take an editor, an editorial assistant or local freelancer for coffee or lunch to 'pick their brain.' Ask lots of questions and allow them to talk so that you can learn from their extensive experience. If they're a junior editor (or, heck, even a sales person) they can still provide valuable 'intel' on the specific needs of their outlet, who the decision-makers are, and who's who in the editorial department.

If you are passionate about a certain niche of travel – indigenous culinary experiences, women's rugby, kayak camping, Amish quilting, eclipse travel, or something else – then work to meet others with that same passion, be they editors, other writers, tour operators or agents. Odds are a connection with someone in your niche will lead you to others – any one of which might need a subject matter expert writer sometime, or who could serve as a source for your future article on 'Australian Travel Agents Specializing in Eclipse Travel'.

But where do you find these elusive editors? Many smaller and mid-sized publications list staff on the website, or you may need to dig around to find emails for specific people. Even a generic 'info@' or 'editorial@' email is better than nothing. If you find a name, you can research online too, especially via LinkedIn. To narrow your search further, sign up for TravMedia.com, which aims to be the 'LinkedIn of the travel industry.'

After all, everyone you meet has the possibility to open another door for you, someday.

Assess Associations

There are a multitude of professional associations within the travel industry, large and small, vague and specific, nonprofit and for-profit. Research to find associations that serve your specific area or niche within the broader travel industry spectrum. Narrow that list to a few organizations you could join. Then do more in-depth research: Interview current members, read financial statements/annual reports, download the literature and research their programs, and talk to representatives at events. Build a spreadsheet, if that's your thing, to compare them side-by-side (as best you can).

As a longtime travel industry association guy, I can tell you there are good and not-as-good associations. Generally, the not-as-good ones have some sort of leadership issues: the Board of Directors hasn't kept a good focus on the organization's trajectory or the Executive Director's stayed in that position far too long. Both these situations can lead to an organization that has gone 'stale' and isn't producing exceptional, effective programs and opportunities for members. Dig into their website. Is it itself stale, confusing, dated, and/or just a 'hot mess'? That's an immediate sign of issues. Download the annual report (if they are a nonprofit, as for-profit associations won't generally produce one) and compare membership and annual meeting attendance year-over-year. If either have been declining, that's another red flag.

Once you've completed your research, you should then pick one (no more than two, if you're really tempted) and dive deep. Apply, get accepted (membership fees for freelance writers are often deeply discounted), then connect with the association staff to ask your questions (after all, as a member they now work for YOU). Become a (respectful) regular contributor on the social media platforms. Attend local networking meetings, and budget time and funds to attend national/international conventions. Volunteer for positions you're comfortable with, that play to your personal skill-sets and will get you exposure, whether that's Associate Vice Chair of their Ad Hoc Instagram Launch Committee or a 'captain' of a single convention pre-tour group.

Twelve years working on staff for travel associations helped me develop a large network of contacts, including a slew of travel writers and editors. I reach out to many of them with pitches and story ideas as a real, trusted friend, as opposed to some unknown attempting a cold pitch. And, as a member of the Society of American Travel Writers (SATW), I've had articles run in major U.S. publications because I attended various SATW events, met editors, listened to what they had to say, and then pitched ideas within the scope of their publication.

Attend Events

Go. Get yourself out there. Events are tough, but make the time, expel the energy, and be a consistent attendee at local events local and, if you're able, national and international.

Attending an industry trade event isn't usually cheap: Membership fee, registration, and travel.

It's an investment of money and time in your future as a writer. Some associations offer discounts or event scholarships for young, new, or specific types of members, or they may need volunteers and may wave registration for someone who's willing to work throughout the event.

If funds are tight, then focus on events closer to you and investigate more affordable accommodation options like hostels or crashing with a friend. Don't sacrifice access to the event to save a few dollars though – if you find a cheap place to stay, but it requires an hour and three trains to get to the event location, you're going to have a challenging time.

At the event, be proactive. Introduce yourself. Strike up conversations. Heck, chat up vendors and sponsors if you need to, as they can all be a valuable part of your network. After you build a rapport, you'll be surprised who they also know.

A sidebar for all of you introverted, passionate, deep-thinking writer types: I hear you. I'm one too. I'd much rather be at home with a book or sitting at a café with one good friend rather than face the gauntlet of 'cold starts' at a new show where I know no one. But you have to get over your fear of small talk and rejection, and get the heck out there. Make a goal to strike up conversations with 4-5 people at each event. Then follow up and stay in touch. In my career, I went from a person that barely had the nerve to approach anyone at a new event to a person that is now (mostly) confident getting on stage before several hundred people to emcee entire conferences. Start small if you have to but just starts – even if it's just one person at a time.

If you meet one person at an event and strike up a good relationship, you haven't met one person, you've met 1xX people because that one person knows X more people they can introduce you to and smooth that transition. Everyone you meet has the possibility to open a door for you, someday.

Go on any appropriate familiarization (fam) trips, pre- or post-tours, educational, or free of charge trips. Some of the best ones may fill up quickly. Some people registering for a travel conference claim that pre-tour events were 'just for fun.' But that's missing the point: You'll get to know other industry professionals on the pre-tour, go beyond simple 'networking' to straight-up, travel-buddy bonding and, if things go well, roll into that show with brand new friends. And those friends are 10xX in terms of introductions at the show.

Also, good writers' events often have a panel of editors talking about how they like to be pitched, their process for evaluating pitches, and what they're looking for in the future. Attend these sessions and drink in their knowledge and advice.

Find a Mentor/Mentee

There's no shame in reaching out to someone senior in the industry and politely, professionally inquiring if they'd be open to mentoring you. Doing so shows you crave knowledge, seek advancement and are proactive – and that's (still) rare. So, you have nothing to lose as even the act of asking makes you look good. And if your potential mentor says 'no,' they may think about who would be a better fit for you and connect you with other possible mentors.

Seek out people who are experienced and knowledgeable about the industry (specifically the sector of the industry that you are interested in), and compassionate enough to give up their time to help. This will take time, and you have to build a network and evaluate prospects before asking and eventually finding one that's a good fit. But you certainly won't find a mentor if you don't start.

When you're more experienced, you can return the favor and offer mentor someone junior. And, that junior person can provide new intel, leads, suggestions, and directions from their own company, or the industry at large.

Don't Be a Twit

You'd be amazed at how many people, in any industry, don't or can't comprehend this concept. Screwing people over ('destroying a bridge') might get you a short-term win, but it's going to be a long-term loss. Even an annoying intern you dress down in an email might someday turn out to be an editorial assistant who's assigned to review your initial pitch or contributes to a decision to buy your story.

At one of our associations, we had a member who was a podcaster. She was smart, talented, aggressive, creative and produced quality work. She was also selfish and would often pitch people on 'partnerships' when she was actually asking them to pay money to sponsor her podcasts. She cut people off, offended people, and just generally didn't play nice with others. I couldn't ever recommend her. I wouldn't take a trusted contact at a brand and then subject them to working with someone like her. When another friend said she was going to take a job doing sales for the podcaster, I had a frank and open conversation about why she should not work with that person because she was just too difficult and offensive.

Don't seek short-term, immediate personal gains at someone else's expense. Play the long game with honor, integrity and thoughtfulness. Treat everyone with kindness and respect. It will pay itself back on you a hundred-fold in the long run.

After all, everyone you meet has the possibility to open a door for you, someday.

❋ ❋ ❋

'Chez' Chesak is a travel writer, 15-year veteran of the travel industry, executive director of the Outdoor Writers Association of America, board member of the Society of American Travel Writers, and co-chair of the Planning Committee for their annual Convention. Learn more about his work at www.chezconnects.com.

PAYING IT FORWARD: A WRITER'S GIFT TO HIM/HERSELF

Mentoring new writers and sharing work with writer friends isn't just a great karmic gift, it's a way to bring sustainability to your own work.

By Jo Ostgarden

Writing work and opportunities have life cycles. Sustainability is the key to keeping you in the flow. Sharing work connections and contacts can keep working coming your way during dry times, help keep you humble and, also incidentally celebrates the great circle of the writing life.

Building strong reliable connections with a wide pool of writers at every level of skill offers many other benefits: By sharing work and connection, you'll discover greater efficiencies, more effective output and the chance to leverage mutually beneficial opportunities. Shared work also promotes reliability, support and recommendations
from other writers or editors.

New writers, in particular, need to consider sustainability. Keeping work flowing and payments rolling is the only way this life works if you want to make a living at it. Unless you can spend all of your time traveling and sniffing out new articles and angles, there are bound to be down times.

Sustainability is something long time writers are well aware of in all its iterations. But sharing work and contacts (editors, agents, publishers, destination marketing organizations, hotel marketers, and the like) is far from intuitive. Holding tight to your "insider info," often feels like the only way to hold off the competition. But let's face it, there are times when you can't do the work—you lack the time or resources, or the assignment's destination or subject matter is just not your cup of tea or expertise.

Having connections with other writers who might possess either/or and being able to recommend them to an editor, publisher or DMO is a pathway to sustainability. It also is a karmic gift. At the end of the day, you never know when an in-kind recommendation will come as a favor returned.

The person receiving this gift should definitely meet your standards. It will reduce disappointments for everyone involved. Even so, recommendations carry risks, and can sometimes even backfire. That writer friend may have less than admirable deadline standards you aren't privy to or may have a lot of personal chaos going on. Hopefully, the editor can separate you two in his or her head, but often they won't or don't.

Money Can Royally Mess Things Up

I am reminded of a young woman I hired as a day-work 'nanny'. I was working on contract for a guidebook, as an editor for a magazine and as an assignment editor for a new online city guide – from a home office with a child just old enough to trigger complications around that scenario.

The young woman I hired had just graduated from a prestigious private college with an English degree, and had spent a good deal of the previous year traveling. I offered her some easy but fast and furious travel assignments focused on some of those destinations she had visited.

Despite some required Level 3 and 5 editing, her work ethic and enthusiasm impressed me. Everyone has to start from somewhere right?

As time went on her work improved and she eventually left me to freelance, and to build her freelance niche. I recommended her work to a friend who was an editor at local newspaper.

After my book was published, the publisher told me they were looking to another guidebook with a foodie focus. The contract terms and the turnaround time weren't for
me. I well understood my limitations. The publisher asked me if I knew anyone else who could do it, but also indicated he planned to pay them even less than the fee he had shared with me.

I asked my former nanny-writer friend if she was interested. Of course she was!

Before she emailed him back, I carefully coached her on book contracts and payment. I told her what the publisher had offered me and advised her to hold fast to that price.

She certainly could get it. She deserved it, and had the skills and the expertise to cover the topic. Despite the gap in our experience, it wouldn't hurt me to have her get paid the same as I would or someone else of my experience would command.

Shortly thereafter, she emailed me and told me how excited she was to take his offer (mic drop) at less than half of the fee he had told me he planned to pay. She then informed me she would have done it for free just to have the opportunity. Of course, that's what some publishers are counting on... and why they hire good editors.

In her favor, over the years, he did contract her to do an additional edition of the book. She also leveraged those books to do several others in the same category. So happy ending, right?

Not so fast.

Over the years, I have seen the price drop on contract work for similar books. Is this the downstream effect of new writer's settling for less just to get published? It could be. I have heard countless stories in recent years of travel writers being pitted against 'influencers' in the race to acquire travel opportunities. There's a long history of "pay to play" scenarios where writers are asked to write travel articles in exchange for destination assistance, but only if they can trigger a deluge of "likes," "shares" and website visits.

Recently, I turned down a travel guide for a well-known publisher when I learned they were having a number of writers compete with each other. Each potential writer for the book was required to produce a full-blown editorial and marketing proposal for the book. In the end, only one would be chosen from among us, but the publisher would also have all of their marketing and editorial proposal work laid out for them to decide upon – for free.

I also turned down a guidebook from a publishing company that planned to pay zero royalties and half the price I had been paid for a previous travel guide of the same size and complexity eight years earlier. They were offering zero travel support for a project that would require driving at least 2,500 miles (if one were to start by flying to the starting destination) over several weeks (gas, meals, food). It just didn't make sense financially. No assistance for marketing either. I would have had to shoulder that cost as well.

These are just a few examples of the downstream effects of what happens when writers isolate themselves in solos. Like anything, there's power in numbers. You also need to be careful about recommending writers whose standards you're unsure of, or who may not understand how their decisions might trickle down to others.

As one longtime travel writer friend remarked after I shared my past ordeals: "To love is to risk your heart. But to offer work connections to others is a risk to your reputation.

You need to know that they care as much about you as they do about getting ahead or making money. Some of it comes down to trust and communication – everyone has hidden motivations."

The Art Of Trust

Indeed, there is an art to work recommendations. Yes, there is some required peeling back of motivations ahead of referrals and sharing. It also means being honest with yourself and others about expectations. Being accomplished in your skills and abilities, and being reliable only works for you and your reputation; but it can extrapolate to the people you recommend.

And it also goes the other way: don't forget where your recommendations come from. Be worthy of them, be honest, be reliable and have your writer friend or mentor's back. They likely have something invested in that recommendation, and, ultimately, so do you.

Despite some of things I have experienced, I still believe in sharing or helping other writers with contacts and work connections when the opportunity arises. Just make sure you communicate. Reinforce your common bond with careful listening and expectations, understanding each other's values and motives, and the potential outcomes.

Of course none of this can be effective if it's just a temporary strategy to get one or the other person something they want. Before you recommend someone or ask someone to recommend you, take time to reflect on your principles and values to make sure they're an integral part of your work ethic and work share.

* * *

Jo Ostgarden has traveled the globe by bike, plane and train. Editor and principle writer of the 17th Edition of Best Places Northwest travel guide, she has an MA in journalism and decades of reporting experience primarily in health, wellness and outdoors adventure travel.

HOW TO BUILD RELATIONSHIPS WITH PRS (YOUR LIFELINE TO A LONG CAREER)

There's one very important factor in the equation that leads to a long and fruitful career in travel writing – your relationship with public relations (PR) people.

By Lindy Alexander

Quite simply, PRs are some of the most important people you need to connect with (and stay connected with) if you want to be a successful travel writer.

The good news is that PRs in the travel industry are usually happy to meet and speak with travel writers. To make initial connections with PRs, contact your local tourism bureau (for example, if you live in Sydney it will be Destination NSW, or if you live in Portland it will be Travel Oregon). The title of the person you reach out to may vary from organization to organization, such as: 'media and marketing' or 'global sales' or 'PR specialist', but essentially their roles will be similar.

Developing a relationship with PRs takes time, but if you focus on building and maintaining your relationship, it's a connection that will be long lasting and will take you many places (literally!)

And remember, the PR world is a small one and word travels fast. If you are a reliable, courteous and engaged freelance writer who regularly delivers quality content, you'll be in demand.

Getting invited on your first familiarization trip

From the outside, it can seem like there is a magic formula to getting invited on a familiarization (fam) or press trip.

There are two kinds of fams – one is a group fam that you do with other media such as journalists and editors, and the other is where you travel individually and seek support or sponsorship from tourism bodies, PRs, individual operators and hotels.

Generally speaking, you'll need a few bylines under your belt before you can get sponsorship or hosted travel because, at the end of the day, it's expensive for tourism bureaus, PR agencies or brands to cover the costs of airfares, accommodation, experiences and food for writers, and they want to make sure you can deliver an excellent return on their investment.

The best way to build relationships and get invited on your first press trip is to ask to meet up with a PR for a coffee to learn more about their destination, products and experiences and their current focus (e.g. some will have key experiences or destinations they want to highlight in the coming 12 months).

Online hubs like TravMedia are another great place to connect, and make sure you register for events like IMM (International Media Marketplace) – a single-day networking event where travel writers, editors and bloggers meet travel and tourism brands and PRs in 22 x 15 minute one-on-one appointments.

It's always a bonus if you're a member of your national travel writing association, as this shows PRs you are a legitimate travel writer.

Once you have met a PR, ask to be put on their media list to receive press releases, but also let them know which publications you write for so they can consider you for upcoming group fam trips/press trips.

The best way to get your first individual fam is to link it to a place you're already going. For example, if you're travelling somewhere for a family holiday, and there's a bunch of new vegan eateries that have opened in the last three months, pitch an editor and if they commission you, then approach the city's tourism board to see if they would host you at some or all of the eateries.

Working while on the road

Doing work while you're away is really about prioritizing.

I've been on trips with freelancers who, instead of staring out the window while they are on a bus between destinations, open up their laptop to work on a story. Other freelancers do work for the first couple of hours during a flight and then have the rest of the time 'off'. I've also been in Ubers with freelance writers doing interviews on the way to the airport (not to mention free-lancers who are paged over the loud speaker and nearly miss their flight because they are trying to make use of the airport's wi-fi before they board a flight).

Working while you're away will also usually mean uploading images and stories to Instagram or making use of a free hour to check out an aspect of a destination or hotel that you can later write about. And lots of your work while you're on the road will be taking detailed notes, snapping photographs, collecting business cards and making voice recordings so that once you get home you have a thorough collection of memories to write rich, engaging travel stories.

Making the most of your trip

If you're serious about being a travel writer, even if you just want to do it part-time, you'll need to make the most of your time on the road.

Many beginning travel writers have dreams of long-haul flights (business class please) to exotic places, but savvy travel writers know you don't necessarily have to travel far to be a travel writer. In fact, leveraging your knowledge about your hometown or where you currently live is a perfect way to get started.

I broke into travel writing (and food writing) by focusing on new trends and new restaurant openings in my hometown. For the times when I had to travel, I aimed to get one story for every day I was away. That worked for my first two trips and then I sadly failed to meet my target for nearly every trip after!

After speaking to different freelance travel writers from all over the world, many aim to get one story for every two-three days they are away. Of course, this will depend on where you are going and the kinds of experiences you are having, but generally I've found this rule of thumb is a great one to aim for.

The best way to get as many stories out of a trip

Have at least one commission before you go (most of the time you won't be 'allowed' on a press trip without having a firm commission be-forehand – although this does seem to vary de-pending on which country you live in).

Have a 'cheat sheet' of publications and their specific sections (e.g. '24 hours in' or 'the best places to eat and drink' or 'meet the local') – this will help you brainstorm ideas.

Write down all your ideas while you are away, even if they're not fully formed. I often create a space in the back of my notebook for different story ideas that occur to me while I'm away.

Do research beforehand. If you're going on a group fam trip, don't rely on the PR to do all the research for you. Look at the places you are scheduled to go to – and if you'd prefer to do something else that would make a better story or an additional experience, let the PR know. I've been on trips where writers have opted to do different half-day tours because that would suit their publication's audience better.

While you're away, speak to locals about what else is happening in a destination; as the ones on the ground they'll often be able to highlight new trends or interesting phenomenon – you can often get new story ideas this way.

I recently travelled to Canada for a week (Saturday to Saturday) and at the time of writing this article, I had written and been commissioned to write four stories (with one pitch waiting for a reply).

My cornerstone experience that I was commissioned to go on the trip was about the Rocky Mountaineer from Vancouver to Banff. That was an 1800-word story for a glossy women's magazine.

We had one night and one morning in Banff, so I also pitched a story about where to eat, drink, stay and play in Banff for the digital site of one of Australia's premier food magazines.

Over dinner one night I was sitting next to one of the Canadian PRs and she mentioned that the Rockies were becoming a popular spot for 're-laxation tourists'. I asked her what kinds of activities were popular, and then I pitched a story about five ways to unwind in the Rockies for an online site of a popular travel magazine.

We also spent one day and a night at a mountain lodge, so I pitched and wrote a story for a national newspaper's travel section about the Nordic spa experience at the lodge.

Keep in mind that in each of these pieces I made sure I mentioned the Rocky Mountaineer. Even though I was keen to generate as many stories as possible for me financially, I was always cognisant that the Rocky Mountaineer sponsored my trip – they want to get the maximum return on their investment.

But don't be downcast if you can't spin as many stories as you'd like (or as you expected) – sometimes trips and schedules don't go according to your plans or hopes and sometimes what you think will be a great story ends up being a flop.

Lastly, make sure you keep in touch with your PRs and let them know where you're up to – communication is key. Even if you're pitching stories with no luck – let them know. They understand that it can be a fickle industry and that sometimes it can be hard to place a pitch.

* * *

Lindy Alexander is an Australian freelance travel writer who regularly contributes to international and Australian publications such as The Australian, The Sydney Morning Herald, Travel + Leisure Southeast Asia and The Telegraph. Lindy is the founder of The Freelancer's Year – a popular blog that helps fellow freelance writers write, earn and thrive.

KINDNESS KILLS

Don't let the violent imagery of this oxymoron confuse you. Personal decency is a freelancer's most effect-ive weapon.

By David Mumpower

T he math of content creation is simple. In even the least competitive fields where you'll find a lot of potential work, you're unlikely to claim the title of best or most tal-ented writer. In an industry with only 100 po-tential freelancers, only one percent of the job force can be the best.

It's a numbers game, one that you'll lose.

How can you stand apart? You can be everyone's friend, even to the clients who make you mutter under your breath or delete angry replies before you give in to aggressive urges and hit send.

I speak from experience here. I've been my own

boss for about 20 years now, and my boss is re-lentless and utterly lacking in pity. That dude never gives me a day off. I work weekends and holidays. I'd sue if I didn't have to look the jerk in the eye every time I stumble across my reflection.

Making peace with myself was the first step in becoming a successful content creator. I had to address the gigantic, kid's-letter-to-Santa-sized volume of flaws in my character and try to neg-ate enough of them that I'm no longer my own worst career enemy.

In my earliest days as a writer, the internet was the Wild West, and I had more than a few gun-fights. I wrote angrily and aggressively, which led to some burned bridges. A few years ago, I got diverticulitis and had a gruesome surgery that left me on my back for six weeks. It gave me plenty of time to reflect on my shortcomings.

Taking Stock

That surgery and subsequent grueling recovery helped me become a better person and, acciden-tally, a better freelancer. Humbled and painfully aware of my mortality, I took stock of where I could do better. One of the primary ways was to mimic my father more.

Dad was almost physically incapable of saying no to people in need of favors. Not coincidentally, when he passed away, he was mourned like a tribe elder. Others he'd met along his journey recounted stories of his generosity until the funeral home literally starting asking that people leave. The eulogies might have lasted into the morning if they hadn't.

What can we all learn from one person's munificence? Even when you think nothing of a gesture, you make allies when you demonstrate kindness. Others remember such actions long after you do. Being a Yes Person is also a strong character trait in and of itself.

Why should you try kindness? Have you ever seen the movie, Charlie Wilson's War? It recounts the story of a Texas Congressman in the 1980s who almost accidentally won the Cold War for his country.

Wilson was oddly positioned to sponsor bipartisan legislation. Many of his fellow members of Congress owed him favors. Why? Since the Texan's district didn't ask much of him, he had a rare ability to say yes to people who needed his vote to pass other bills.

In his own words, Charlie Wilson was owed more favors than anyone else in American politics during the 1980s. He cashed in all of his credits in exchange for military support in foreign countries hostile to Russia.

Ignoring the nuanced diplomatic aspects of this historical footnote, think about what's important here. An anonymous congressperson's impact is felt to this day on the world stage.

And it happened because he tried to say yes when others were inclined to say no. It's a valuable lesson about the power of positivity, one that could filter into your professional life.

Accidental Expert

One of my primary avenues of travel writing stems from an oligopoly. Only a handful of businesses in the entire world sell this niche product, a kind of Disney hotel timeshare. Through this venture, members can pay in advance for several decades of Disney resort stays. The content that I've created for one company in this industry has led to a great deal of work with others. I've almost accidentally become one of the foremost experts on the subject.

In a field that has less than ten primary vendors, I've worked for more than half of them. In other words, every time I've attached my name to my writing, a competitor in the field has noticed what I've done to the point that they sought to hire me, too. Had I shirked my duties and cut corners with my writing, I'd have significantly less business today.

I've gotten many gigs almost accidentally, including a multi-book deal. One of the reasons why is that I try to do favors for other people whenever possible. Over time, I've been what some would describe as lucky. I choose to believe that the universe takes care of its own.

When a client approaches you for some work, think of the situation as a networking opportunity. Find a way to say yes, even when your real answer is no.

I'll give you an example. A client from the aforementioned oligopoly recently approached me with an offer for contract work. As a new business, they couldn't meet my quote yet.

Rather than dismiss them out of hand, thereby leaving them feeling diminished, I went out of my way to give them a direct method to contact me. Simultaneously, I provided advice regarding several startup business concerns of their industry that I'd learned over time.

As a fledgling organization, this potential client had no direct knowledge of certain parts of their industry. It cost me literally nothing to take a few minutes out of my day to offer some suggestions. Some freelancers might embrace the maxim that time is money and cut the conversation short once the finances fell apart. Instead, I worked to build a bridge, seeing them as a long-term ally.

I've seen no immediate benefits from this action on a personal level. However, I later found out that the founder of this company previously worked with a different client. Unbeknownst to me, they had a conversation about my professional acumen that I'm confident will have beneficial ripple effects to my career.

I gained one of my most valuable clients in this same manner. This corporation's business manager read my work on a competitor's site. In my writing, they recognized exactly the sort of content that they sought to produce.

When this organization offered me steady work, they made no attempt to lure me from the other client. They knew from my writing that I'm not a person who will ditch someone for a better offer at first opportunity. It was this very aspect of my personality that appealed to them. Their pitch was a joint proposal that allowed me to continue my content creation for a direct competitor of theirs. They didn't try to poach me but rather generously suggested that I work for both of them, something that the other client happily allowed.

From my original business partner's perspective, I had written work that was so good it triggered feelings of jealousy with their competitors. Who would want to lose that person, after all?

Looking To The Future

My final piece of advice is the Trojan horse approach to leveraging now for the future. When I can't accept a job, I try to connect the would-be client with a friend whose work that I trust. I will suggest up to three other freelancers who I know can fulfill the customer's needs.

I know from experience that when I set up an ally with a steady supply of work, this friend will attempt to repay the favor at some point. Even though I've technically said no, I've laid the groundwork for a future negotiation.

With an associate working for a business and putting in a good word for me, I'll have no problem finding later work. And again, this benefit transpires because I've said yes when an overworked professional's instinct is to say no.

I won't delude you into thinking that unearthing freelance travel gigs is easy. Instead, what I'll say is that you can improve yourself as a professional and as a person by demonstrating kindness and saying yes more often. You'll discover myriad benefits of this behavior that will bleed into all parts of your life.

❉ ❉ ❉

When David's not at Walt Disney World, he's writing about travel, movies and box office analysis, economics, streaming media, technology, and parks & recreation. He's the author of the Disney Demystified and Behind the Ride book series.

PITCHING, CREDENTIALS AND 'THE SELL'

FOREWORD BY JAMES DURSTON

One of the commonest fears among new freelance writers is the pitch: that email you send off to your favorite publication containing not just the great idea you've been saving especially for them for months, but also your hopes, dreams and any sense of self worth. The fear of rejection is probably the second-biggest fear in the freelance world, just behind the fear of being ignored altogether.

This chapter's aim is to a) show you what a good pitch looks like - feel free to copy the structure in your own pitches; b) provide one way you can make your pitches stand apart and become extra appealing to an editor; and c) provide a step-by-step case study of a newbie travel writer who started at zero, but now regularly sells travel stories. It also aims to help all those who are pitch-phobic to get over that fear, and get over the sense that each pitch is a delicate piece of art that requires weeks of planning and second-guessing. Winning assignments is as much a numbers game as it is a game of thoughtful construction. So while it of course pays to think about what will appeal to each editor and publication you target, it pays just as much, if not more, to push out those pitches on a weekly - even daily - basis.

So why is knowing how to pitch important? Pitching is the only way freelancers can get the stories they really want to write in front of editors. Once you become established as a writer and editors trust you, work will find you without your pitching efforts. Take John Malathronas as an example, in the Q&A article in this chapter. With many years and hundreds of bylines under his belt, editors now often pitch him to write the stories they need. That's an excellent position to be in. But John still finds time to pitch editors himself, a) because the work that comes directly from editors won't always pay the bills each month, and b) that's how he gets to write the stories that excite him. Being a pen for hire is great, but it means you're always writing someone else's ideas. Pitching well gives you a good chance of writing your own ideas - the stories that matter to you - as well.

The first Travel Write Earn book *How To Sell Travel Articles: Advice From Editors* goes into the fine details of good pitching, and the Travel Write Earn pitching workshop (available on the TravelWriteEarn.com website) dissects one of the best pitches I ever received as a commissioning editor. But John also gives examples of a pitch he now finds embarrassing and one that he thinks worked well - heed those and you won't go far wrong.

The best way to write a slam dunk of a pitch is to have a really great idea - read the chapter on 'Finding Ideas' for insights into that rather nebulous concept. But there's another, easier way to make your pitch emails stand apart: with photos. Photography or some visual element (videos are particularly important these days, as are infographics) is pretty much standard for every travel article published today. If you can help the editor out by offering to source pictures yourself or providing your own (if they are of a decent quality) you make your 'package deal' all the more attractive. PJ Heller describes how he uses his photography not just to sell articles, but to inspire article ideas too.

Selling articles requires more than a great pitch though. And selling articles regularly - getting *picked* over all the other travel writers pitching your editor that week - requires what I have coined the *PICD* formula:

1. Write a great **P**ITCH
2. That contains a great **I**DEA
3. Backed up with great **C**REDENTIALS
4. And conclude with a great **D**ELIVERY

We've seen what goes into steps 1 and 2. But the trickiest part of this formula for brand new travel writing rookies is step 3: the credentials. How do you get experience, when people won't hire you without experience? This perennial chicken-and-egg scenario plays out for hundreds of people every day - and there's no silver bullet. If you're serious about being a credible, professional freelance writer, there's nothing you can do today that will get you hired tomorrow. But there are several things you can do over the next two, three or six months that will get you hired regularly in the future. Deborah Mackie had this exact problem, and in her article we see the steps she took to start building that experience and her credentials, so that eventually an editor will look at her portfolio, see her bylines, see the communities she is a part of, the blog posts she writes and the experience she has developed and feel assured that when hiring her they are getting a bona fide professional who will do a good job.

That after all, is all we can hope and ask for. So start today, start now, and start well, and it won't be too long before you too will be able to give pitching advice to others coming along in your wake.

* * *

James Durston is a career journalist, managing editor, author and entrepreneur. Formerly senior producer at CNN Travel, he now runs the Travel Write Earn blog and coaching site, as well as Pitchwhiz, a platform that connects journalists with publications, organisations and editors that need content.

HOW TO PITCH: THE GOOD, THE BAD, THE UGLY

Without a good pitch, your sterling copy may never get printed. Expert travel writer John Malathronas describes his strategy for winning assignments

J ohn Malathronas is the author or co-author of 20-odd travel books, including various Rough Guides, Michelin Green Guides and other tales of his travels, from Brazil to Singapore. His byline also appears regularly in various top-end travel publications such as the Sunday Times Travel Magazine, CNN Travel, National Geographic Traveller and more.

All of which makes him a perfect sounding board

for those looking to do what he has done so well. Here he explains his methods for sending winning pitches to editors.

You're an experienced travel writer now - do you still need to pitch like you did when you started out? What has changed if anything?

Yes, like everyone else, I still need to pitch and expand my client list, if only because even the most trusted of editors can disappear. They may switch to a job with a more limited budget, change desks from travel to lifestyle which is not my area, move from print to online where different rules apply, overspend their budgets or of course, get sacked or resign altogether. Once four of my regular editors disappeared within the space of a month – from a mixture of the above reasons – and left me gagging for work.

What percentage of your pitches win assignments? How has this changed over the years?

I estimate 5 percent early on in my career, but I can tell you exactly from 2012 onwards. It was then that I developed an Excel spreadsheet which allows me to track what I pitched to whom and when (to follow it up 1-2 weeks later). Reading it now, out of my first twenty pitches in 2012 three were accepted. Two of them were 'cold', that is to people who had never heard of me before. Out of my last twenty pitches, six were accepted and none of them were 'cold'.

However, one of these pitches was an idea that I'd already sent to three different editors who'd rejected it. The fourth one thought it was a good match for his audience. I think it's important not to give up if you have a good idea and to circulate it to various people over a period of time before you give up on it. You should be mindful of where you pitch, of course. A tour of Bauhaus sites in Germany may be good for the Daily Telegraph but it won't wash for Travel Africa.

Do you have a template or 'formula' you follow when pitching and can you describe it?

Not a template as such, but yes, I have a 'formula'. I think you need a catchy headline, a short in-depth description of the pitch that is tailored to the publication, and finally a reason why you are a good match for the story.

A headline can be catchy for many reasons but an anniversary like the moon landings say will certainly catch the eye of an editor. Something new like a new attraction will also work. This all requires a lot of proactive research.

A good match for a story is never "I'm going there next week". If you've been offered a press trip then the editor you're pitching to very likely knows about it and has either commissioned it already or isn't interested. If you're going to an unknown corner of La France Profonde and speak fluent French, have written a guidebook and several articles about the country then you are a good match.

Do you pitch for every pay packet you bank? How else do you ensure an income?

Once you develop a relationship with an editor then you get contacted for assignments that have been planned by the desk you're working for. This is particularly noticeable in magazines that work under strict deadlines and plan most of their content months in advance. For instance, once I established a relationship with a well-known magazine, I was sent to Japan, to Austria's Christmas markets and on a Danube cruise for specific features they had already chosen. However, in order to achieve such trust, you need to spend a long time – and we're talking years not weeks – cultivating a professional relationship. Plus of course there are guidebooks whose updates ensure a regular income of sorts. These are, however, drying up at the moment.

Can you recall any pitches that make you cringe now? What would you change?

I keep all my pitches on file, so I'll dig one out. This is my third pitch to one national newspaper in 2006. It was an on-spec pitch, that is, I'd written the article beforehand.

30th anniversary of the Soweto riots

Here is a piece for you in case you want to include a travel feature for the 30th anniversary of the Soweto riots (June 16). I have just come back from Soweto and I am writing about the township from a traveller's point of view 30 years afterwards. It is offered to you on a First British Serial Rights basis at your standard rate (photos separately considered).

There are four problems with this pitch, even if I thought that sending the article along removed any necessity to expand. I doubt if the editor ever opened the Word file. No catchy headline, no description of the content (except for the cringingly obvious "I am writing about the township from a traveller's point of view 30 years afterwards") and of course no reason why I was the right person to write it. (In fact, I'd written a whole book, "Rainbow Diary", about South Africa that had been published by Summersdale only a year earlier.)

But the worst part was the timing. I sent this email on May 6 for an anniversary happening on June 16. I should have sent the email three months in advance. I didn't get a response, quite rightly. Note also the by now almost obsolete BSR reference. You may still find it useful if you're pitching to a magazine that doesn't publish online. There are still some.

Can you recall a pitch that worked surprisingly

well? Describe it.

This is my second pitch to a national magazine that was accepted in 2016. I'd just met the editor at an event and we got on very well, so I pitched to her immediately afterwards.

Shoulder Season Santorini: Seven Things to do in Santorini in September
Explain why best season for Santorini is September: fewer tourists, lower prices, sea warmest after the summer.
Then a para each on:

- *Watch the sunset from Oia (July-Aug it's a scrum).*
- *Shop for jewellery at Fira (will find a nice jewellery shop).*
- *Have a cocktail at Franco's (chic bar-with-a-view).*
- *Sunbathe on the black beach at Perivolos (out of several black beaches this is the best).*
- *Take a boat cruise in the caldera (swim by the newly formed volcanic islets).*
- *Go wine tasting (there are several wine estates and Santorini's Assyrtiko dry white wine is excellent).*
- *Visit the mythical Atlantis at Akrotiri (this well-preserved Palaeolithic village is said to be the mythical Atlantis).*

I speak fluent Greek and I am the co-author of the Rough Guide to Greece and the Rough Guide to the

Greek Islands.

< followed by links to my books and several articles on Greece>.

I think this is a very good pitch. The headline is alliterative (to the extreme), the outline body shows I know exactly what I'm talking about and I let the editor know why I am the right person for the job.

Is there a publication you've pitched and really want to write for but haven't been able to crack? What do you think the reasons are?

I'd love to write for Atlas Obscura. I have the hardback, I subscribe to their email lists and I'm totally tuned into their mindset. I've had three pitches rejected but very politely. The editor has kindly encouraged me to persist and I will. I just haven't found a subject that interests them sufficiently.

What publications seem easy to win assignments for and why?

I've found no publications easy to win assignments for. I just think that people go straight for the nationals without having honed their pitching skills first. They fail and get demoralized. If anything, competition for such articles is fierce. Start by pitching something lower down the food chain and only when you become reasonably experienced – especially in your pitching –

consider the nationals.

One final 'must do' piece of advice for early-stage pitchers?

Do not ever offer to write for free. "Building up a portfolio" doesn't wash, because we all know which publications pay (and therefore have more stringent standards) and which don't. By all means showcase articles in your own blog or website, but never write for free for others – unless they are friends. Not only will you continue to write for free in the foreseeable future, but you'll also undermine others in our profession.

* * *

John Malathronas is the author or co-author of 20-odd travel books, including various Rough Guides, Michelin Green Guides and other tales of his travels, from Brazil to Singapore. He blogs at malathronas-.com.

THE IMPORTANCE OF PHOTOGRAPHY FOR TRAVEL WRITERS

Freelancers who can write and photograph are invaluable to editors. This skill set combination can lead to future assignments as a writer, a photographer or both.

By PJ Heller

When you think of San Francisco, what comes to mind? Probably the Golden Gate Bridge. What about Sydney, Australia? The Opera House. And when you envision Paris, you're likely to picture the Eiffel Tower.

Such iconic images have been used ad infinitum to illustrate travel articles in books, newspapers, magazines and online. Just as a travel writer strives to describe a location in a new and interesting way, images showing new and unique sites that accompany those stories can often make the difference between acceptance and publication by an editor or the dreaded rejection letter.

At the very least, being able to offer imagery to accompany your story will be a great boost to your pitch if it means you could save the editor some work and/or budget.

"We're looking for images that move us. They are authentic, spontaneous, and in-the-moment – our photography is captured, not planned," notes World Nomads, a website that features travel stories and photography while promoting its international travel insurance and travel safety services.

For the travel writer, there are numerous options for obtaining imagery, ranging from the do-it-yourself approach to sourcing stock photos to partnering with a professional photographer.

Most people are content to whip out their mobile phone and snap photos of what is in front of them. More than 1.2 trillion images were captured globally by smartphones and cameras in 2017, according to InfoTrends. And in some cases, such as in a remote, off-the-beaten-path location, carrying a smartphone rather than a bag filled with camera gear may be the only viable option. But be aware of two things: 1) Don't be dull! Try to give your photos life and energy. 2) Use an editing program, such as Camera +, Snapseed or Lightroom, to bring out the best in the images.

Tip #1: Shoot the interesting stuff

The key is avoiding shooting the mundane. Instead of simply photographing people strolling down Las Ramblas in Barcelona, look for creative ideas in and around the stores, eateries and the popular La Boqueria public market. Or try focusing on the colorful murals and artwork lining the narrow side streets. Get closer, show details, include people in your photos, and seek to capture the essence of the location.

"Get lost. Wander down alleys. Sit in cafés and watch life pass by. Don't eat where the tourists do, but where you see locals. Set off down a street and see where it leads. Look around the bends, over the rises. Get away from the crowd," advises Robert Caputo in the National Geographic Photography Field Guide.

"To me, photography is an art of observation," says noted photographer Elliott Erwitt. "It's about finding something interesting in an ordinary places . . . I've found it has little to do with the things you see and everything to do with the way you see them."

The same can be said for evocative travel writing.

If shooting everyday things, such as monuments, statues or buildings, is critical for the story, try to capture those scenes using different angles or at different times of the day or night. Include people in the photos.

Tip #2: Keep practising

The ideal situation is for travel writers to spend time honing their photography skills. Not only will that allow them to capture imagery that best illustrates their stories – rather than having to spend time searching elsewhere for those photos -- but can earn them more money when they offer a complete package of self-generated material.

When I wanted to focus on my photography, I queried a major Midwest metropolitan newspaper that had advertised for a West Coast writer and asked how they were going to handle imaging needs. That led to several photo assignments to illustrate articles written by others. I subsequently pitched them a story I wanted to both write and photograph and they gave the go-ahead.

From that point on, they assigned me to either write and shoot a story or to provide images for articles written by others.

Tip #3: Don't buy all the gear

Travel writers needn't obsess about photo equipment. As photographer Peter Adams notes, "Photography is not about cameras, gadgets and gizmos. Photography is about photographers. A camera didn't make a great picture any more than a typewriter wrote a great novel."

Tip #4: If your photography is horrible, don't despair

For those who do not want to bother shooting photos, numerous stock photo agencies such as Getty Images, Shutterstock, Zuma Press and Alamy may have the images needed. But searching for the right photo can be time consuming. Getty, for instance, has more than 200 million images available; Alamy has some 160 million images on file and is adding 100,000 more each day. Zuma, the world's largest independent press agency and wire service, has more than 20 million images online.

You can also look at the tourism department's

website, which often will have a section dedicated to high quality imagery of the destinations they want to promote. Or of course you can try the hotels, restaurants and other operators, companies and organisations, especially the bigger ones, who may have press images available as handouts.

Dwarfing those collections are the images on social media: an estimated 350 million images are uploaded daily to Facebook alone and 100 million photos and videos are uploaded each day to Instagram. Warning: They are not free for the taking.

Tip #5: Be aware of rights

Images posted online and on social media may be copyrighted and using them without permission can prove costly. If you see the perfect image online or on social media to accompany your story, contact the photographer or agency to find out details about licensing the photo. Numerous websites do offer free public domain images or images under Creative Commons (CCO).

Tip #6: Consider collaborating

Another way travel writers can obtain the photos they need for their stories is to team up with a freelance photographer. The advantage of this approach is that the writer is free to concentrate on the story while the photographer can capture the images that best illustrate the article. Good communication between writer and photographer is essential; they can either work together on location or the writer can pen the story first, then provide a copy to the photographer so s/he knows exactly what to illustrate.

If there is a downside to this approach, it may be that with today's shrinking markets and shrinking budgets, an editor lacks the funds to pay for both a writer and photographer.

Regardless of the approach, excellent photography is a key to selling any travel story.

"The whole point of taking pictures is so that you don't have to explain things with words," Erwitt says.

Notes photographer Mark Denman, "When the world asks 'what was it like?' Only the photographer can say 'see!'"

✤ ✤ ✤

P.J. Heller is a photographer/writer with bases in both America and New Zealand who loves roaming the world on assignment ot in search of unusual stories and photos. His background includes work with the wire services, daily and weekly newspapers and for more than two decades on a freelance basis. He is a contributing photographer to the Zuma

*Press photo agency with his work published world-
wide. He can be contacted through his website at
www.photoreporters.com.*

GETTING THOSE INITIAL CREDS: IT TAKES TIME TO BECOME AN OVERNIGHT SUCCESS

To become a successful travel writer that editors will consider working with, sometimes you need to invent a whole new persona.

By Deborah Mackie

It can be tempting to look at established travel writers and see only the glamour of free travel to exotic destinations, invitations to the best events and a high life of fine food, wine and extraordinary experiences. Spoiler Alert: This is not where I tell you that it was quick and easy or that it all came to them through a lucky break. Ask any one of them and the answer will be the same: they had to get their start somewhere – and it almost certainly wasn't a by-line on the cover of a glossy magazine.

Travel writers follow different paths. Some start off part time while holding down their real job; others are already in an associated field when they decide to morph into travel writing. Some, like me, start from scratch.

For me, the starting point was the decision to reinvent myself in retirement. I had been a journalist in a former life and I now had the opportunity to travel extensively. I decided to combine my love of writing with my travel experiences. I could write well and I had some exciting tales to tell. I'm a great storyteller and I was passionate about sharing my travels with others. In my naivete I assumed that would be sufficient: all I would have to do is write good copy and publications would want to publish my scintillating travel tales – and they would pay me for it!

There were many things I didn't factor into my equation for success, but my biggest mistake was not addressing the question of "Deborah Who?"

Editors are inundated with pitches and submissions and in this book there is a wealth of experience and advice to help you get your work and ideas in front of the right people at the right time. But I found the biggest hurdle was not just getting my story in front of an editor, but getting them to give me a go. I was an unknown quantity; I had no published work to point to and I had no connections.

That's when I realised that I didn't just need to reinvent myself – I needed to create myself. I had to create "Deborah Mackie, Freelance Travel Writer". She had to have a profile; she needed connections in the industry; her name needed to sound familiar; she had to provide proof that she could write; she had to show she was widely travelled and had exciting stories to tell; and she had to present as someone who was professional and serious about her craft. Deborah Mackie, Freelance Travel Writer had to appear successful before she had had any success at all.

Step 1: Learning the Basics

I enrolled in a travel writing course – on-line with weekly modules comprising audio lectures, printed reading material and assignments where all classmates could see your submission and feedback was provided to the whole group so that everyone benefited from the input.

This was an invaluable investment on several fronts. Not only did I learn so much about what really happens behind the travel writing scene, but I also learned that there were so many angles to travel writing, so many opportunities and niches that I hadn't even considered.

Step 2: Coaching

My next step was to engage a life coach/image consultant. This might not be for everyone, and it can be expensive, but I'm a big believer in self development and to me the investment was well worth it. These sessions helped me crystalise exactly what I wanted to do; what I wanted to be. "Being a travel writer" is a very generic, vanilla description and I knew I wasn't going to get very far if I was content to be a tiny fish in a mass market of generalist writers. With the help of my coach I drilled down to identify what type of travel writing I wanted to focus on, who I wanted to write for, what travel really meant to me, how much of my recently retired life did I want to spend on this venture, and what did I want to achieve as a travel writer.

Step 3: Social Media

I don't have a technical bone in my body and I was terrified at having to come to grips with all the technical aspects of modern business life – and I knew I had to overcome these fears if I was to create the modern, successful business woman called Deborah Mackie, Freelance Travel Writer.

I started with LinkedIn. I registered a few years ago but had not been back on the site. I had less than 10 connections – all family or friends – and I knew I had to reach the magic '500+' to appear legitimate, successful and connected.

The reality of LinkedIn is that there are some people who will consider you unworthy and will ignore your request to connect. Thinking about it from their side, why would a successful travel writer or editor with 500+ connections want to connect with an unknown wannabe with very few connections?

I developed a strategy that enabled me to organically grow my number of connections and broaden my network. I started by reaching out to people and organisations who would benefit more from the arrangement than me – they were looking for people to help their cause and the fact that I was little known would probably be less important to them. I targeted PR people promoting destinations, venues and experiences; tourist bodies promoting their city, country, state or region; tour operators and guides in locations around the world.

My self-imposed rule is that I send a message with every invitation to connect explaining who I am and how I think we might have common ground. I am also fastidious about sending a quick thank you note to each person who connects and leaving the way open to work together in the future. It is also my rule never to reject any invitation to connect – it is always in my mind that we all have to start somewhere.

Once I collected a reasonable sized base of connections, I then started to supplement that with invitations to more journalists, editors, authors and freelance writers.

My strategy worked: the more connections I made, the more connections I made. My acceptance rate started to skyrocket. But it was not quick or easy; such a concerted campaign takes a lot of time and commitment.

Another great aspect about LinkedIn is the ability to publish your own work on the site. I wrote several pieces and posted them online and it not only helped me develop my profile, but it gave me links to online work (something that would prove crucial as I moved forward).

Instagram and Twitter were easier to set up and develop. They both provide a great platform for promoting links to your work or other travel-related writing, and they help keep your name in front of people. But they also come with the ubiquitous lurkers and scammers. My advice is to make good use of the "Block" and "Unfollow" buttons and move on.

Like most people, I had a Facebook page but I realised I needed a more professional face on this platform. Not everyone who was interested in reading about my travels wants to see pictures of my family, pets or cooking efforts.

Step 4: A Website

I accepted that I couldn't attempt the technical challenge of setting up a website myself, so I engaged a local expert. This meant I had someone who could design what I thought I would need and who could also advise me and teach me how to actually use it. A website can provide a range of profile-enhancing features: I could write and post my own stories, ones that weren't necessarily destined for mainstream travel publications; I could provide a wealth of value-added information and links to my readers, such as upcoming events and travel tips; and the site includes direct links to my other social media sites. My website turned out to be one of my most productive and beneficial investments.

Step 5: Get Published

Don't get too excited. I don't mean that after following steps 1-4 I suddenly had travel editors clamouring for my work. What I did have were opportunities to have my stories published on non-paying travel sites. I know this is a big no-no for many writers, it was a necessary step for me at the time, I thought. I chose the sites carefully and made sure I submitted my best writing. Just because I was doing it for free didn't mean I wanted my name forever attached to sub-standard work. The big benefit was that I created more links to published work.

Step 6: Join the Writing Community

No matter how many social media platforms I

had, no matter how many digital friends, followers or connections I'd made, I couldn't develop my profile unless I was positively engaged in the writing community. It became startlingly obvious that the more I interacted with others on the various platforms, the more they engaged with me. I became part of conversations, my name was in front of people, my connections expanded.

I started to join various writing groups and associations and that was when I realised the importance of having those links to published work - it is often a prerequisite for joining some groups.

It was also at this stage that I discovered the generous spirit of many in the writing community. There are so many established travel writers who provide valuable on-line resources free to their followers: books, lists, contacts, databases, strategies and advice that I was able to access to help me in my travel writing journey.

Step 7: Mentoring

Once I had what I considered to be all my basic infrastructure in place I then decided to bring in the big guns. I invested in mentoring. I engaged a couple of different but equally established players in the travel writing space to mentor me. One was a well-known Australian freelance writer and the other was a former editor of a major travel writing outlet. I have the benefit of their ongoing expertise and feedback on everything from identifying stories, fine tuning my pitches, editing my copy and accessing their contacts. No, it's not cheap, but I don't think I could put a value on knowing that their help, support and advice is so easily accessible by email, phone or skype.

Did It All Work?

By following all the steps above, I created Deborah Mackie, Freelance Travel Writer. When she submits a pitch, even when that editor has never heard of her before, they can look at some examples of her writing, they can check out her website, Instagram and Facebook page and see that she's always travelling to interesting places and searching out experiences with a difference. They can see she's a member of various groups and associations and she knows many of the people that the editor knows. Maybe she's worth a try. That's the aim of my game – to get the editor to give me - the newbie - a go.

It's been a big investment of time, money and commitment to get this far, but I decided I wanted to be a freelance travel writer and I'm playing the long game.

At the time of going to press I've got quite a few irons in different fires and I'm confident that I'll have an ever-increasing number of by-lines to my credit before long. I've done everything I can to establish my initial creds but there haven't been enough nights yet to know whether I'm going to be an 'overnight success'.

It's Not Published Until It's Published

Once you do get those initial breaks, it can still be a very frustrating game; for all travel writers, not just newbies. You might think you have a commission or your piece is just about to be published or you've established a good relationship with an editor who is going to give you your break. Then it doesn't happen. Editors change ... publishing schedules change ... budgets change ... people move on to new jobs ... marketing organisations lose contracts to produce magazines ... airlines pull out of a market sector and your piece is no longer relevant for their inflight mag ... people agree to be interviewed and then turn coy ... organisations or interviewees become so controlling about the content of your article, it's no longer worth the angst ... your magazine contact that you've worked so hard to cultivate gets overruled by their boss ... editors are just so busy they don't get back to you about your pitch, or they fluff about for so long that your once highly topical piece loses its allure and gets dropped in favor of the next big thing.

These are just some of the many reasons why it takes so long to get those initial runs on the board. But is it all worth it? Definitely!

* * *

Deborah Mackie is a travel writer based in Canberra, Australia. She travels extensively and is constantly seeking angles around food, wine, people, out of the way destinations and out of the ordinary experiences. She turned to travel writing after retiring from careers in journalism, marketing and law - which gave her the nose for a story, the eye for a saleable angle and the discipline of detail and fact checking. Follow her work at deborahmackie.com and on Twitter: @DeborahMackie5.

BLOGGING, SOCIAL MEDIA AND AFFILIATE MARKETING

FOREWORD BY JAMES DURSTON

The writing world used to be a simple place. There were writers over here, publishers over there, and between them they put words and books out into the world. It was pleasingly linear. But then in 1990 the "world wide web" was invented and the publishing industry exploded in a million-billion different directions. This publishing Big Bang created a new universe, in which words and ideas were transported thousands of miles at near light speed to anyone who cared to click.

The world of blogging, social media, influencing, and content and affiliate marketing might appear overwhelming to anyone who has only looked upon this brave new publishing world from afar. But it needn't be. More importantly, the internet era comes with many-fold more opportunities for travel writers to earn supplemental income as they ply their passion.

Blogging, for instance, is no longer simply a way to write a digital postcard to friends and family members, keeping them updated with your latest travels, gardening projects and life events. Blogging is now an established and popular livelihood, earning many individuals five- and six-figure incomes each year. But how do they do it? How do they make money from their blogs? Ashley Howe describes one way in her article about affiliate marketing. If you have or can create a blog that attracts regular visitors, you can also be a sales channel for many brands trying to connect with new customers. Ashley explains in fine detail how to do that.

There is often a line drawn between blogging and freelance journalism or travel writing. Travel writers are the editorial professionals who get published by the big broadsheet newspapers, inflight magazines and high-paying websites. Bloggers are essentially failed writers, not good enough to be published by anyone but themselves. This is an outdated and inaccurate perception. Many if not most prized, professional writers these days also run their own blogs, if nothing else as a way to promote themselves and their writing that has appeared elsewhere. Fiona Maclean's article explains exactly how she runs a professional writing business while also running an income-generating blog, and gets the best of both worlds.

If you have a blog that attracts a high number of regular visitors, you may start to encroach into the transcendent world of 'the influencer'. Invariably tied to high social media followings, becoming an influencer ensures you 'never have to pay for a hotel room again', according to one influencer I know. That's not exactly true. There has been a backlash against entitled influencers recently, with some hotels publicly shaming individuals for trying to blag free accommodation in exchange for a tweet or two. But it is true that brands, travel brands especially, such as hotels and airlines, will often see value in offering free services in exchange for social coverage. Shobha George's article details the questions you need to ask yourself, and the research you need to do, before you decide to go down the influencer track.

Speak to any brand manager who has worked with influencers, and you'll hear one word mentioned even more than "followers" - "engagement". It's no good these days to have 100,000 followers on your social channels if your posts don't attract comments, likes and shares. Rossana Wyatt's piece explains why this is, and how to write engaging posts.

Finally Betsi Hill explains, once you have a following, how to use each social platform for maximum effectiveness, and Sue Reddel gives an in-depth and highly detailed case study of her work on Twitter, creating "Twitter chats" that become engaged communities that can then be used to generate income.

The internet and social media world offers so many ways to create, engage and monetize what you most likely do already. This chapter reveals the details of some of the easiest ways you can start to do that right away.

* * *

James Durston is a career journalist, managing editor, author and entrepreneur. Formerly senior producer at CNN Travel, he now runs the Travel Write Earn blog and coaching site, as well as Pitchwhiz, a platform that connects journalists with publications, organisations and editors that need content.

AFFILIATE MARKETING: HOW TO EARN GOOD MONEY DOING VERY LITTLE

Affiliate marketing is a great way to earn extra money. Travel bloggers are particularly well positioned to take advantage of this 21st century revenue stream.

By Ashley Howe

A ffiliate marketing can be a lucrative opportunity to earn money for travel bloggers. You may have heard bloggers referring to affiliate marketing. This chapter will explain what it is and how you can use affiliates to monetize your site. The good news is that it's pretty straightforward to get into, and you have almost certainly come into contact with a blogger who is using it to make extra money. This means that it works as a way of generating income. Additionally, I have worked for an affiliate coupon code website, and as an account manager for an affiliate network in the past, so I have seen the benefits of affiliate marketing first-hand.

What is affiliate marketing?

In short, affiliate marketing is when a brand pays an 'affiliate', which includes bloggers, a commission for selling products to their audience via a special link.

There are four main players in affiliate marketing. The publisher (or affiliate), the consumer, the affiliate network, and the brand.

The publisher is the person who is looking to earn money from affiliate marketing. In this case, that's you. The consumers are your audience and site visitors. The affiliate network is the company involved in tracking sales. The brand is the company selling a product or a service.

What Are The Benefits For Travel Bloggers?

Affiliate marketing is something that every travel blogger should have in their arsenal. The main reason is that it can be a passive income. Once you've added your affiliate link or banner to your blog post, homepage or social media, it just stays there. That means that if your readers click through to buy something on an old blog post, you've made money without even trying. However, as with everything, the more promotion you do, the more money you could make.

According to one study, 49 percent of consumers depend on influencer recommendations, and 40 percent go on to buy if they saw that recommendation on Facebook, Twitter or Instagram. This means that bloggers do have sway when it comes to influencing purchasing decisions.

Sometimes, companies will give out exclusive offers or coupon codes for websites with a high volume of traffic or high converting websites. This means you will have a coupon code for your visitors only, which means you can give your readers some extra value. It's a good way of building up trust with your readers. When I worked at coupon site Flipit we got given an exclusive coupon code by one of our advertisers and the website started to rank on Google. The site got a good reputation and people trusted it because the site was giving them working coupon codes for discounts they couldn't find anywhere else.

What Kinds of Companies Use Affiliate Marketing?

So many different kinds of companies use affiliate marketing as a way to boost their sales revenue. It's not only reserved for fashion or clothing. In the travel niche, there are companies like airlines, travel insurance companies, hotels, booking sites, tour companies, credit cards, cruise companies, car rental companies, and experience websites to name a few.

It's important to think about what products your audience is interested in when you're looking at which products to promote. Travel blogger Anna Karsten from Anna Everywhere was getting lots of questions about the clothes she wears from her readers, so she has an article on finding cheap clothing that contains affiliate links. Travel blogger Nomadic Matt uses affiliate links for some of the businesses showing on his resources page. They include tour companies, transport, job resources and blogging resources.

How Much Can You Earn?

This is a difficult question because there are so many variables. For example, it can depend on your audience size and your engagement, what your travel niche is, where you choose to promote something, how often you promote something, whether your followers like what you promote, how many products you promote, or how you promote something.

As an example, the blog Making Sense of Cents made around $50,000 in July 2019 from affiliate marketing alone. Many make far less, depending on their audience (we're talking $20-100 per month). Generally speaking, how much traffic you get and how engaged your followers are is a good indication of whether or not you'll make good money. Usually, the more traffic you have, the higher the earning potential.

However, your audience doesn't have to be huge if you have a niche and heavily engaged followers. For example, a travel blog that focuses on drone photography could be quite lucrative because drones are a high-value product. If you are earning a 5 percent commission on a $1,500 order, you'll make $75. That multiplied by however many people make a purchase could be very profitable.

Commission Rates

Commission rates and commission structures

vary between advertisers and what works best for their product. As a rule, credit card companies offer a dollar or euro amount, and things like flights and hotels will have a set percentage of the full purchase amount. These are some of the relevant terms that you might come across

CPA (cost per action) - a percentage of the total sale value
CPL (cost per lead) - a set dollar amount
CPC (cost per click) - a set price per click

In my experience CPA commission rates can range from 2 percent to 20 percent depending on the type of company it is. For set dollar amounts, commissions can be anything between $10-200, depending on the product. With airlines and electronics, because their margins are low, their commissions always err on the lower side. I've seen commissions between 1-2 percent for these items. Clothing generally tends to be in the 10-15 percent range, and Amazon has a whole list of different commissions for different products. Make sure you do your research though, as sometimes commission rates vary between networks (sometimes by up to 3-4 percent.)

So How Do You Start?

There are a number of different and creative ways you can incorporate affiliate marketing into your blog or social media channels.

Links: The first, and most obvious way is to incorporate links into a blog post or social media post you're already writing. Maybe you are reviewing a suitcase that you know is on the Amazon affiliate program, for example. This makes it easy for you to add an affiliate link into your content. You get these links from the affiliate network or brand, through their affiliate marketing programs.

Banners: Banners can be placed at the sides of your blog. Advertisers provide the banners that they want to use, and it's just a case of adding the embed link to your sidebar.

Package deals: Working with a brand on a package deal is probably the most lucrative way of earning money. In cases where you have a large, engaged audience, often brands will send you something for free, and pay you (sometimes at a lower rate because they will pay you commission for every sale you make) to write an article or create a social media post, or a combination of the two that includes their product or service.

Paid search: Some brands allow paid search on their brand name. You put up the initial cost of running the paid search, and then when people buy things you earn a commission. If you know what you're doing, this can be lucrative, but it is risky as there's no guarantee that people will go through and buy.

When I worked at the coupon site we did a combination of all of these apart from banners to try and capitalize as much as possible. There was a blog attached to the site, so we regularly did things like Christmas gift guides. We also asked for commission increases or exclusive coupon codes for prime positions in our newsletters or on our website. Do whatever works with your website and think creatively.

Top Affiliate Networks and Programs

There are so many brands with affiliate programs - some of them create their own affiliate program on their own websites, and some work exclusively with affiliate networks. Others do a mix of both, so it's important to compare commission rates when you are joining an affiliate program.

Some brands with their own affiliate programs:

- Amazon
- Expedia
- Tripadvisor
- Groupon
- Booking.com
- Airbnb
- Lonely Planet
- SkyScanner

These affiliate programs have their own user

interfaces. In my opinion, they don't usually look as slick or give you as much information as the affiliate networks. It can also mean that the brands are harder to contact and work more personally with because there's no way of messaging them. However, one big advantage of working with a brand directly is that their commission rate might be higher than their commission rate for the affiliate network and if you're big enough they might contact you directly for promotion opportunities.

The other thing to mention is that if you have been searching for an affiliate program for a particular brand on the affiliate networks and you can't find it, try messaging them on social media to see if they have their own private program. This is how I managed to get Interislander (the ferry between the North and South Island in New Zealand) to work with us on our NZ coupon site.

Affiliate Networks

Affiliate networks have relationships with multiple advertisers, often in several different countries. Some of these affiliate networks charge a small fee to publishers (that's you) for joining up, and they sometimes have a vetting process to make sure that your website isn't spammy. In my experience, the more information you have about an advertiser, the better. All of the affiliate networks will tell you what the commission rate is. It's also useful if an affiliate network tells you what people are buying through your website. This can help you to make decisions on what you promote. Knowing a company's conversion rate can be useful - if you know your clickthrough rate (how many times people click from your website to theirs), you can work out roughly how many people will convert.

This is a list of just some of the affiliate networks that are out there. There are plenty more, and some are of a higher quality than others. It also depends on where you are in the world.

- APD
- AWIN
- ClixGalore
- Commission Factory
- Rakuten
- Skimlinks
- Shareasale
- Tradedoubler
- Viglink
- CJ Affiliate

So now you know what affiliate marketing is, and how you can use it as part of your success plan, start shopping around for affiliate networks and programs to get started with. Good luck out there!

* * *

Ashley is a freelance copywriter. She has worked in affiliate marketing both as an account manager at an affiliate network and as a manager for several affiliate marketing websites. You can find her website here: www.ashley-howe.com

FREELANCER VS BLOGGER – CAN YOU BE BOTH?

Choosing between blogging and freelancing doesn't need to be a stark this-or-that selection. Here's how to wear both hats successfully.

By Fiona Maclean

There's a myth in the blogging and free-lance writing world that the two are distinct vocations. But in my experience it's possible – and, for some people, desirable – to do both. There's also a third category, namely 'contractor', that dovetails nicely into the kind of portfolio career that gives you the freedom to travel, but provides income. For me and many others, it's simply a question of getting the balance right.

Control The Mix

As a blogger, I am 100 percent in charge of how my income is generated:

- I can pitch for sponsored posts and trips, which is a great way to generate content while also pursuing my passions.
- I can run advertising on my site to provide a regular and reasonably stable income.
- I can establish affiliate partnerships and generate income when someone buys as a direct result of a link from my site (see the separate chapter for the details on this).
- I can run courses, write ebooks and generate income from the sale of that content.

Many bloggers do a mixture of some or all these things. With total control on the mix and on the amount of time I spend working on the blog, I have a greater level of control over the amount of income generated.

The downside? My only support is a network of other bloggers (or my long-suffering partner). And, I'm somewhat at the mercy of the networks where I promote my content. So, if there's a major Google update, I can see my advertising revenue fall. If Instagram changes their algorithm my engagement will drop, and I won't get the same sponsorship deals. Each one of my affiliate partnerships has the freedom to change their payment structure or even to give up working with affiliates altogether. It can be both unpredictable and lonely.

Making Money

As a freelance writer, I am paid a set amount for the number of words I produce. It's up to me to pitch features and sell them to magazines and papers and it's up to me to invoice and chase payment. But what ends up in print or online isn't always what I've submitted, and although I generally love getting a by-line, on some occasions I don't want to be associated with the finished feature. If I want to travel, I need to get an editor's commissioning letter before I go – something that can be like drawing blood from a stone. As for invoicing and chasing funds, I am the world's worst!

Rates have stagnated as print media struggles to survive in a digital world and as the digital world is flooded with online content. It can be hard to break-even on a press trip, let alone make any money.

Of course, it's possible to freelance in other areas too. Freelance social media management for services and brands, freelance SEO (search engine optimisation) and freelance PPC (pay per click - a form of internet marketing) management are all areas I will consider for the right client with a flexible approach that will fit with my lifestyle.

Finally, there's contract freelance work, which is where I started more than twenty-five years ago. When I accept a contract it's usually for a fixed term and it pays a day rate. I've worked from home and in client offices, and a mixture of the two. Usually, I've been hired to support a launch or special event, so there's a finite term I'll be working for. Usually, contract freelance work pays well – rather better than the permanent equivalent – because the employer is expecting you to hit the ground running. It also lacks flexibility. I've found myself doing less contract work as my blogging business has grown. It works well for some people though – one of my colleagues looks for a freelance contract in the UK for the South African winter and for one in South Africa for our winter. When she's not contracting, she pitches and writes freelance features. And, she keeps her own blog running too – enjoying the opportunities that brings to travel and review.

What Works For You

How should you decide your own path? The best thing about all these ways of generating an income is that there is no right or wrong. I'd advocate a mix and match mentality.

Of course, if you see your blog as the main income-generating vehicle, you should invest as much time as possible working on that. You might choose to take an easy, low-pressure contract or work freelance as a Virtual Assistant while you build up that business. Or, if you can afford to do so, you might set yourself a window to get everything started, with, for example, a six-month sabbatical from working for other people.

In my case, I love writing my bog London-Unattached, but I also get a lot of joy from writing for other people. I see the two activities as symbiotic – the content I get from trips with London-Unattached is reworked into features that I can sell to magazines. And, that helps my blog because I get a backlink from the publication which helps to establish me as an expert.

I use contract work in two ways. Firstly, I have one contract client who provides me with a regular small income. We've worked together for so long that he's totally flexible about how I do my tasks. And in return, I provide extra support when it's needed to cover for holidays for example. Secondly, if I'm offered a lucrative short-term contract, I'll drop everything and do it, treading water with the blog for a period.

Will I ever work full-time on London-Unattached? Perhaps, if I lose my current client. But I suspect not, more because I'm (nearly) old enough to retire. In another life, I'd have done things differently. And that's the joy of this style of working – you can do what suits you.

* * *

Fiona is a London based freelance writer, blogger and marketing consultant. Fiona has over 25 years of freelance experience working for major companies including Vodafone and British Telecom. She was part of the dot-com boom and set up a portfolio of online dating sites in her 30s, selling them for a seven-figure sum just eighteen months later. She is also the founder of an award-winning blog that has evolved into the online lifestyle magazine, London-Unattached.com.

ENGAGEMENT, NOT FOLLOWERS, IS THE KEY TO SOCIAL MEDIA SUCCESS

The new era of 'influencing' is upon us. If you can get your followers to engage with your content and social channels, opportunities await.

By Rossana Wyatt

If one word captures the digital media mission of recent years, it's 'followers'. How many you have, how many more you could gain, and how to gain them quickly. But having thousands of followers really means nothing if they just sit there doing nothing. I see so many accounts with great numbers, but when I look to see how often they are being engaged with, it is surprising to see how little it is.

It is certainly easy enough to purchase large follower numbers; there are tons of programs selling new followers for every platform. There are even some unethical tactics (so-called 'black hat' techniques) that go against the SEO guidelines, used to increase site rankings to try to get more people to click over to their blog.

Many of these large followings do not drive any kind of engagement, as many of them tend to be bots - software programs, not real people - and therefore you don't get actual eyeballs on your content. If you are working hard at creating content and sourcing information, don't you want actual people to see it?

The reality is, you want your content to be good enough that people keep coming back to your social profiles and your blog because they love your content, and want to engage with it.

Engagement - The Key to Social Success

Becoming a thought leader or the go-to source for your niche won't happen if your content is not being engaged with enough either -- but you don't have to have a large following to make that happen. If people are engaging with you regularly through social media, they are more likely to click through to your blog as well. Having a dedicated following (no matter how small) lets others see that people like your brand or content, making them more likely to check you out and follow you because of that.

Creating a community feel for your followers is also very important, no matter what size your following is. You want to create engagement with your followers, but in order to do that, you also must interact with them regularly. Responding to questions or comments, thanking people for sharing, and giving shout outs to your followers to make them feel special should be done regularly.

Think of it this way: let's say you could purchase the same items at two different stores, but the one store made an extra effort to get to know you and find out what your preferences were so they always had items ready for you. Which one would you frequent more often, or make your go-to store? My pick would certainly be the one that wanted to get to know me, and that is what many of our followers want as well.

That is why it is important to create content that really resonates with your audience. Check to see which post topics tend to get more comments, shares, etc., and post more content that includes those subjects.

No matter who you are, the more engaged the audience is, the more it ultimately helps build relationships and trust with your followers. This is the cornerstone of social media.

Engagement Is a Daily Task

And now it is my turn to confess ... in the last 20 months, because of contract work commitments, and other things, I have not spent the time that I should have engaging and interacting with my followers on any of the platforms. Instead of the steady growth that I had seen before, I stagnated, losing some followers and gaining fewer back.

I totally understand this. I used to tweet curated, relevant information 30 to 40 times a day, and this dropped to an average of four to five a day during this period, with some days without any tweeting or sharing of information. I also did not respond or reply as often, nor did I post as often to my other platforms. I was on a time crunch and my social profiles all suffered. Any available time I had, I put toward my responsibilities to my contracts.

Not only did my social platforms suffer through this time, so did my blog. I was not writing as often as I should to keep the blog relevant, because I did not have the time. There were weeks that I didn't even look at my blog. How can I expect a follower to look at it if I didn't? Nor did I add any new articles to it to keep visitors interested and have them coming back for more. My regular visitors didn't see any new material and I was not promoting the articles I already had to send new visitors to the blog.

As I look at my blog stats now, I am amazed that people are still visiting. If I had the time to keep things going, my site visits would have increased over the last year and a half, but I essentially walked away from it. So instead, they fell. Now comes the time to rebuild all those relationships so my followers get to know me again. I must make the time to post relevant information, and to interact with more of them so that they want to engage with me about what I am posting and get that conversation started.

Increased engagement with my followers means that my content is being consumed, it is resonating with my community and it has value, and I am a thought leader and influencer. My followers are based on quality vs quantity and are not just a vanity metric.

Once I regain that trust, the site visits will follow, and, should I want, I will be able to monetize my site with advertising, affiliate marketing and more.

But increasing my followers isn't going to help me now if I don't also build on the relationship and trust with the followers that I already have. Once I do that, then more quality followers will come. Good things take time.

* * *

As a gluten-free lifestyle and travel writer specializing in family and solo travel, Rossana loves discovering new foods and adventures on her journeys as she explores and shares the stories of the destinations she visits. When she is not traveling, Rossana works as a social media strategist, bringing people and brands together. She tweets @RossanaWyatt.

BLOGGING VERSUS INFLUENCING: WHICH SHOULD YOU DO?

Not every writer needs to be a journalist. Here's how bloggers can become influencers, and derive revenue from partnerships and affiliations via their audience.

By Shobha George

First there were writers. Then with the Internet, came bloggers. The term of the moment these days is 'influencer' - and it has big ramifications for how travel writers can earn a living.

Let's get some definitions down.

'Blogger' is easy to define. To be a blogger, one needs to have a blog - a website where you publish original content. Blogs used to be postcards in digital form - a place for friends and family to keep up with your activities. These days blogs are just places that publish content on the internet - many of them businesses - though the term tends to be reserved for smaller-scale, or independent publishing efforts.

An 'influencer' is someone who has a band of followers whose purchases may be guided by what the influencer recommends. The medium the influencer uses can be a blog, but given the growth of social media channels, influencers tend to be defined by their social media followings.

So, a blogger may be an influencer but not all influencers are bloggers.

Which might you be? Which do you want to be? And how do you earn an income from either? That's what we'll explore in this article.

Influencers have inspired much debate precisely because they are explicitly associated with purchasing power. Opinions about influencers range from a recent New York Times article stating that "influencers are the way of the future" to a Forbes story which likens influencers to snake oil salesmen.

Do You Know Your Brand?

As for me, I side-stepped the influencer versus blogger debate and think of myself as a content creator.

I am a blogger, but I don't think of myself as an influencer. I have a travel blog (Just Go Places Blog), geared towards independent family travel. My followers are expats and others who are short on vacation days but enjoy spending time with their families. Our families enjoy sharing travel experiences together and rarely, if ever, just put their children in a kids' club.

Do You Know Your Audience?

My audience is older and well educated so they are also less likely to be influenced than say, the teenage girls who follow Kylie Jenner. She is a true influencer because as soon as she does something, her millions of fans follow suit. That's how she is able to manage a billion-dollar cosmetics company without advertising.

Age, however, isn't the defining factor. Older people can also be influenced. For example, when Oprah recommends a book to her audience, the book is likely to become an instant bestseller. She is 65 years old, and while her audience will range from anything from mid-twenties to 60 years and up, her sweet spot is likely to be people aged 45 years and up.

Once you know and understand your audience, you can angle your content and your messaging in a way that is most impactful, and without alienating people. For example, while I regularly recommend products and write reviews, I like my audience to think independently about my recommendations and judge for themselves if it's an appropriate fit for them. I present information so they can assess the value for themselves. Just telling them to buy something isn't going to work - and may even backfire.

I also think, with so many blogs out there these days, you really need to carve a specific niche, whether it is as broad as family travel or as narrow as scuba diving holidays. Tailor your content to your audience.

There's next to nothing on my blog that would interest a younger traveler who stays at hostels and loves to party, because I focus on cultural activities like museums and fine dining.

Are You In The Right Place?

Once you know who your audience is, you also need to know where your audience gets their information, so you can follow them there and be active on the right platforms.

I know most of my Gen X audience is not active

on social media. Even if they have a Facebook or Instagram account, they are mostly lurkers.

They do read blogs though so that is where I place my content.

So, where might your audience hang out? My teenage children are addicted to YouTube. They are on Instagram occasionally ... and as for Facebook ... what's that? Any blogger and/or influencer hoping to get my kids consuming their content is going to have to factor in these trends.

You will need to do this sort of analysis as well.

Is It Easier To Be An Influencer Or A Blogger?

Both influencing and blogging are hard work. That one photograph you see on Instagram could be, in fact probably was, the result of hours of planning and hundreds of shots. The best influencer photos aren't accidental and they aren't just a pretty picture. They take time and planning and also tell a story.

You should play to your strengths. If you are a good writer, blogging will come easier. If you are a visual creative, Instagram or YouTube may be a better fit. If you have the gift of the gab, check out podcasting.

Whichever platform you choose, your best results will come when you tell your story your way. Authenticity resonates with an audience and that will automatically build trust.

For example, Kendall Jenner was paid $250,000 for a single Instagram post for Fyre Festival which turned out to be a total bust. But she walked away from that fiasco guilt-free and cash-rich, thanks to the Kardashian magic.

How Do You Go About Making Money Online?

Trust and authenticity are key to making money online. If your audience trusts your recommendations, you have a valuable arrow in your arsenal of money-making tools. The Holy Grail for any blogger is having an interested, engaged audience.

Here are 5 ways to engage your audience:

1. **Stick to your brand's ethos**. If you are devoted to eco-friendly products, suddenly changing tack will throw your audience into confusion.
2. **Create a content plan** so that you have a clear direction of what steps you are going to take and when you are going to get there. For example, if Christmas is an important holiday for your audience, start the information flowing for this holiday a few months early. The Hallmark Christmas Channel starts its festive cheer in autumn.
3. **Respond to people's questions** and

comments even if you think you don't have the time. Don't forget the *social* part of social media. Listen to your audience - don't just talk at them.

4. **Be helpful**. People remember if you have been helpful and provided advice that actually worked.

5. **Always connect**. Many people feel camera-shy or awkward in front of the screen. The audience, however, wants to connect with you and the best way to do that is showing them the real you - awkward, goofy, brilliant you.

And, some bonus tips:

Endorsing people or products that you don't believe in is a sure-fire way to turn your audience off. After all the effort you put into building your brand, I don't think any amount of money is worth losing your audience over.

Forget the idea that bigger is better. You don't need large numbers of followers to become an influencer. A small loyal group of followers who will purchase is far more valuable than a large number of people who are 'just looking'.

Keep in mind that pay can vary widely by industry and by social media platform. For example, the fashion industry is known to be a generous paymaster.

According to the Financial Times, on average someone with 100,000 followers on Instagram can get $2,000 for a sponsored post. YouTube pays out about $3-5 per 1,000 video views, so you would need around half a million views to make the same $2,000. Compare: fashion insta-grammers who have a similar number of fol-lowers can get paid up to $5,000 for a single post.

Passive Income Or Active Income?

For bloggers and/or influencers, one of the most profitable revenue generators is also one that takes very little effort - at least after you've set it all up. This revenue stream encompasses product/service endorsements, product/service sales, sponsored posts, brand ambassadorships, advertising and affiliate sales. But no matter what method(s) you choose, you need to be hon-est with your audience about how you are mak-ing money.

Active income comes from project work that dries up once the work stops. For example, a salary you draw at a job is active income, as is money received from sponsored posts and prod-uct endorsements. You work, you get paid, and then you need to work some more to get paid more.

Passive income is revenue that keeps coming

in, even after you stop the initial work. For example rental income in real estate, or on the internet, advertising and affiliate sales income.

The work required for Instagram sponsorship is much like sponsored posts on a blog. The money is great. But they are one-off posts each time and don't lead to long-term passive income. You need to keep doing those posts to keep earning that income.

Also, seeing sponsored post after sponsored post can look off-putting for a reader. No one wants to be seen as a mark that you keep around as a potential buyer of your products. Once again that social part of social media is important - it means readers and subscribers feel like you have a relationship with them.

I personally prefer affiliate sales on my blog (There is a full article elsewhere in this chapter dedicated to affiliate marketing for all the juicy details on that). Why?

- They are a money earner that produce passive income for years to come. Sure, getting something for free, like a complimentary hotel stay, is a nice quick boost to income (in terms of not having to spend money). But I find I can make more money from affiliate sales in the long term. That blog post will generate income for the foreseeable future so long as I keep it current.

- My audience does not feel my opinion has been affected in any way because I have been offered the product/service for free. Moreover, reviewing products or services comes with deadlines from the people you do business with.

- When I pay for my experiences myself, I also have the option of not doing the review if I feel the product wouldn't interest my audience. For example, I stayed at an eco-friendly hotel in Belize that I did not review for my blog. My audience prefers their eco-friendly hotels with a big dollop of luxury. This particular hotel was light on the luxury and heavy on the crunchy granola factor. The hotel was perfectly fine but didn't fit in with my brand. And because I wasn't indebted to them with a comped stay, that was not a problem.

Allowing advertising on your blog is also an easy way to make extra money. How much you make depends on how much advertising you allow. I know people who are making over $1,000 a month with around 50,000 page views. And, remember this is passive income - you aren't doing anything other than driving traffic to your website!

Good luck.

✣ ✣ ✣

Shobha George is a family travel writer and blogger at www.justgoplacesblog.com whose work has appeared in both online resources and in print. Most recently, she has been a contributor to The Family Travel Handbook published in January 2020 by Lonely Planet.

SOCIAL MEDIA AS SUPERPOWER: HOW TO BE A SOCIAL SUPERHERO

In today's writing and blogging world, creating, maintaining, and growing a social media following can greatly expand your opportunities for success. It can be your superpower.

By Betsi Hill

I f you write for publications, editors often expect that you will share not only your article but the publication across your social channels. Why? This is part of their marketing strategy. They want and need your audience on social media to see their content. Some editors will be upfront about this, but even those who are not want to see you promoting your contribution. Doing so can mean the difference between being a one-timer and becoming a regular contributor for some outlets.

When you write for your own publication or blog, you wear many hats. Marketer is one of the big ones. You want to grow your audience and you want more traffic. You also want more visibility to impress PR professionals. How do you get there? You show up consistently on social media and post good content. You don't buy fake followers or likes.

Consistency will let your readers and followers know that you will be there, that you will show up on social media, and on your blog, and that you will be sharing only the very best content with them. You can have all the tools and apps to help you, but consistency is the key that unlocks social media as your superpower.

To become visible, you must have a strategy for

social media. That strategy is not a "throw spaghetti up against the wall and see what sticks" approach. Instead, it is a well-crafted, well considered social media marketing plan.

Crafting Your Social Media Strategy For Growth

At the end of each month I set aside several hours to schedule my social media for the coming month. There are lots of apps for scheduling, but I use Social Bee for LinkedIn, Twitter, and Facebook and Tailwind for Pinterest. Here are some ideas to incorporate into your strategy.

Twitter Threads

Twitter threads are an excellent way to gain more engagement and extend the reach of your tweets. I participate in two professional travel organization threads weekly, and one mixed niche thread per week.

A Twitter thread is a moderated list of tweets that are more likely to interest and engage people. Each Twitter thread has its own rules. Essentially you are adding a link to a list of other tweets. Your responsibility as a participant in the thread is to click and retweet each tweet in the thread or list. You can add comments to the tweets, but do this after you have retweeted the original tweet.

Twitter Chats

Twitter Chats are another way to increase your visibility and followers (see the other chapter dedicated to Twitter chats for full details on these). A twitter chat is a chat around one unique hashtag. The hashtag lets you follow the fast-moving discussion and participate in it. Most twitter chats are scheduled weekly or monthly. They often feature a destination, or a host.

To find relevant twitter chats, Google Twitter Chats (adding your niche). Chats last anywhere from 30 minutes to 60 minutes and are an excellent way to create buzz and gain interested followers. The key is to participate and be highly engaged with others on the chat. I also recommend following all chat participants.

Once you have found a chat you want to participate in, find a chat room you like. I recommend and use Tweet Chat for twitter chats.

Pinterest

Behind Google and YouTube, Pinterest is the #3 search engine for searching SEO keywords. Pinterest is also where many people find inspiration for planning their travel. When Pinterest first began, it was marketed as "digital scrapbooking" but soon evolved into something much bigger. Pinterest is where many people search for inspiration for trips, fashion, home renovation projects and more.

Enter a search term, such as "Alabama travel" or "Top Florida destinations for Families", and the results are a collection of "pins" that each direct to a web page that is relevant to the search term.

As a blogger or writer, Pinterest should be a significant tool in your social media bag. Each time you write an article and have it published, you should create a pin that points back to the article or your website. If I am writing a freelance piece, I only create one pin. But, if I am writing a post for my blog, then I develop multiple pins and schedule them in Tailwind, which is a tool to automate your pins. I also add pins to my blog post so that readers can pin it to their boards. Using this strategy, you will see your traffic increase.

Using a tool like CANVA (canva.com) allows you to design a pin using one of their templates designed specifically for Pinterest pins. You easily upload your photo, put it into the template, add a title and you have created a pin.

When creating the descriptions for Pinterest, search for the most relevant hashtags. For each pin, I add between three to five related hashtags in my SEO rich description.

Instagram

Instagram is the most visual of the social media

platforms. If your niches are travel, beauty, food, or fashion, Instagram is especially relevant. Brands and destinations love Instagram, and so do your readers.

Best practices for Instagram include stellar photos that stand out and are eye-catching. Include up to 30 relevant hashtags. When you include a hashtag in your Instagram post, a selection of related hashtags appear. Best practice is to include a mix of high volume hashtags (with more than 500,000 posts)and smaller hashtags (60,000 posts or fewer) and niche specific hashtags.

For me, a post that has a great picture and a very descriptive narrative do extremely well. Your goal is to get people to engage with your posts.

Engagement

And let's chat about engagement. Engagement is when someone does something on your post, rather than just looking at it - for example clicking to 'Like' it, or leaving a comment, or clicking to the link you shared. To encourage more engagement, when someone leaves a comment, respond back! You are having an online conversation, which takes two. When you are hosted for a press trip, your hosts want to see you on social media. But more specifically, they want to see your followers engaging with the posts you make.

Growing Your Social Channels (And How To Utilize Them To Find More Contacts And Publications)

Becoming active on social media will provide an opportunity to branch out from the niche you usually write in and expand your audience.

Finding More Publications to Pitch on Twitter

Many writers already have social channels, but they are often under-used. Social media brings you exposure to a wide-ranging audience. A larger audience is a potential bridge to more work. I found many of the publications I do work for on Twitter, for example.

In the Twitter search box I would type something similar to "magazines about travel." Once my search yields results, I follow the publication, begin retweeting their posts and commenting on their posts. I may do this for several weeks or a month. Meanwhile I will research and read the publication. If I cannot find information on who to pitch online, that is where Twitter again comes into play.

I reach in a direct message, asking something along the lines of "could you direct me to your editor, and how to contact them?" Because I have been liking and commenting on their posts, these requests are more likely to bear fruit. Once you have the editor's contact information, you can send your pitch.

Connecting with PR Firms and Destinations on Twitter

Using the same strategy outlined for finding new publications, you can also find new destinations to visit and new PR firms to work with. The key is to begin the relationship with no expectations. You want to like and comment on their posts in a thoughtful manner. Once you've established a relationship, direct message them and ask who handles their media relations. Email that person and begin the conversation.

I'm On Social Media But How Do I Grow My Audience?

There is no silver bullet for growing your audience on social media. It takes time to grow your audience. Posting to your channels is important, and I highly suggest using visual media - photos and video. But note: do not give too much information away, because you want your audience to engage with you.

Twitter

For Twitter, the key is posting multiple times a day and engaging with those who comment on your posts, and engaging with other people's posts. For example, I wanted to post something about our downsizing from a house to a boat. I posted a picture with the boat in the background and wrote "On a whim we headed to Annapolis for a spontaneous getaway. And we bought a boat, which became our #floatinghome for several years. #lifeisanadventure." This simple text created a string of comments, each of which I respond to. That engagement leads to people following you, and you are building your audience in an authentic way.

Instagram

Many destinations and PR firms want writers post on Instagram. No matter how small your audience is, visual content is king. You do not have to post on Instagram while you are visiting a destination, but you want to post in a timely manner. I find that I take a lot of photos during the day, and then I will post to Instagram when I return to my hotel that evening. Tagging the destination, restaurant or attraction is important, so search out their handle on Instagram prior to posting. Add relevant hashtags as needed, including the destination, attraction, or restaurant.

Travel, food, wine, lifestyle, and beauty are the best performing topics on Instagram. Growing this platform takes patience and time. When I am not traveling I post three times a week to Instagram and have experienced steady growth.

Visual posts on Instagram can be done with your phone, and editing is important. My favorite editing apps for Instagram and my phone photos are Color Story and Snapseed, both of which are available in your phone's App Store.

* * *

Betsi Hill is a freelance writer & blogger based in Florida. She is often found traveling onboard Saltwater Gypsea through the islands of the Caribbean. Betsi maintains an active presence on social media (@betsihill) and shares her travel adventures on betsiworld.com.

TWITTER CHATS: A FAST ROUTE TO TRAFFIC AND INFLUENCE

Twitter chats are a great way to engage an audience, gain attention, build community, and create another source of revenue. Here's how to build a successful chat from someone who has done it from scratch.

By Sue Reddel

When my partner and I started Food Travelist, a website to connect culinary travelers with brands, destinations, and experiences, we were completely new to online business building. We created our website, wrote some content, added photos, and waited for people to find us. This was not, as you can imagine, a great approach. We didn't have the budget to buy ads and thought there was a better way to get people to know, like, and trust us. Turns out, Twitter held the key.

I first started participating in 'Twitter chats' about travel as a way to gain followers and build brand awareness for our website. Most Twitter chats operate by asking several questions that the "chatters" answer. Participants follow along by using the chat's designated hashtag. That allows everyone answering the questions to see everyone else's answers.

Sometimes, participants add photos or links to enhance their responses. Once the answers start, then chatters also respond to one another. If you continue participating in a chat week after week, you begin to feel a sense of community, because you're sharing ideas, information, and inspiration with online friends. Of course, you start to follow your new friends on Twitter, and they start to follow you.

We quickly gained followers through participating in chats that take place under hashtags like #TravelSkills, #ExpediaChat, #NUTS , and others. We developed a reputation as food travel experts by sharing great photos and stories of our food travel experiences around the world. I always used a friendly, funny tone that opened the door to many side conversations on these chats. And as people got to know me, they began visiting the website and commenting on our posts.

After participating in Twitter chats for about a year, I started getting asked to be a "co-host" on some of them. Being a co-host involves answering the chat questions, liking and retweeting responses, and stimulating conversation. I enjoyed this role and one day thought, "Why can't we start our own Twitter chat?"

The chats that were already out there focused either on travel or food. Some would throw in a question or two about the wrong subject for the conversation or have a cross-topic chat once or twice a year. But no chat was specifically dedicated to culinary travel. We saw an opening and decided to start our chat under the hashtag #FoodTravelChat.

When we started our @FoodTravelist Twitter account, we only had a few family and friends as followers. We now have over 28,000 followers, all of which have actively chosen to follow us. We have not paid for advertising and have not "bought" any followers. These are highly engaged real people actively interested in food travel, which is the best kind of audience when talking to potential sponsors.

After a while, we started a separate @Food-TravelChat Twitter account. So, in addition to our Food Travelist followers, we now also have nearly 10,000 followers of the chat itself. There is some crossover, but not a lot. And these are people who have voluntarily chosen to follow the chat, so potential sponsors and co-hosts know that we have an active purchasing audience interested in relevant products and experiences.

Creating a Twitter Chat from Scratch

Developing such a loyal following and an engaged community doesn't happen overnight.
Our goal was not only to become the first food travel Twitter chat but also to create a community. We wanted a place where people would be able to share their food travel stories, become friends, meet in real life (if they wanted), and perhaps one day travel together or share a meal. Our website echoed this attitude, tone, and point of view, so driving traffic to specific articles via answers on the chat was a natural fit.

From the beginning, we wanted to bring in relevant brands and destinations that we could feature as sponsors. We knew this would be difficult for a relatively new website and a brand-new Twitter chat, so we opted to work with brands that would provide us with free products to give away during the chats as an incentive for people to participate.

We didn't want to abuse this approach. We didn't want to gain an audience of people who were only interested in winning free stuff. We limited ourselves to a sponsored chat once every few weeks. Because of our active participation in food and travel trade shows, we were able to call upon some of the brands we met there. We asked if they'd be interested in giving us some products to give away in exchange for sponsorship mentions and links. Fortunately, a few agreed. We tailored the chat topics to align with each sponsor but kept them broad enough to encourage full participation.

For our first sponsored chat in May of 2014, we worked with an RFID-protected wallet company. They provided us with several of their wallets as giveaways. After promoting the chat on our website and on Twitter, we ended up with 29 'tweeps' on the chat. Although we were originally disheartened, we stuck with it. Week by week, the numbers started to grow.

A few weeks later, our next sponsored chat featured Brownie Brittle. We talked about "Travel Snacks," gave away two baskets of Brownie Brittle goodies, and had 37 people on the chat. The added bonus was that we asked people to follow us and Brownie Brittle on Twitter to be entered into the random drawing for the prize. This helped both us and our sponsor gain new Twitter followers.

Folks kept returning to the chat and started to become regulars. After a few months, we had begun to find our tribe. While sponsors were a great addition, we didn't need to give away something to get people to join in the chat. By July of that year, we did a sponsor-less chat on "Dining Alfresco," and 81 tweeps cheerily chatted away with one another. We now routinely get hundreds of chatters and upwards of 15 million timeline impressions each week.

As participation in #FoodTravelChat grew, so did the job of keeping things moving and making chatters feel welcome. So, I enlisted a few of the friends I had made on Twitter through previous chats to become moderators for our chat. Their job was to help share announcement tweets of the upcoming chat. They also engage with other participants during the chat to ensure that everyone felt welcome and part of the community. While we could not pay the moderators, we'd send them some swag, like a Food Travelist logo shirt and some fun travel goodies we pick up at trade shows.

Some of our moderators have changed over the years. A few of them have been with us since we started the chat in 2014, and we cherish them. We publicly thank our moderators in every chat and encourage chatters to follow them. This provides recognition for our moderators, adds strength to the community feeling, and helps moderators find reasons to drive traffic to our site.

Expanding Our Growth

Creating a Twitter chat consistently at the same time every single week was important to us from the very beginning. We didn't want people to wonder when the next chat would be. There is no doubt that running a weekly chat is a lot of work. Creating topics, questions, and graphics for the chat is a weekly job. We can spend five to six hours on the technical set up and another two or three on promotion each week. Of course, answering questions from chatters, reaching out to prospective sponsors, keeping moderators informed, and maintaining a presence online are ongoing chores that take a few hours each week.

Managing the @FoodTravelChat Twitter account in addition to the @FoodTravelist account does create extra work. I use this account for promoting the chat early in the week and answering people's questions. It also acts as a home for announcements and provides another way to point traffic to the Food Travelist website. While it may be considered an adjunct to Food Travelist, its focus is on the Twitter chat and so does not publish content of its own.

In the beginning, I didn't share the questions with anyone. I've changed that approach this year, and many people enjoy scheduling their tweets ahead of time or getting their photos ready before the chat. To drive more traffic to the Food Travelist website, I now post the questions every week on a page on FoodTravelist.com that is dedicated to #FoodTravelChat. We share the link to that page several times in our tweets.

We keep the chat questions open and inviting so that everyone can participate. For example, the Hong Kong Tourism Board sponsored a chat. But because not everyone has been to Hong Kong, we broadened the topic to include all sorts of "Asian Feasts and Finds."

This provided an opportunity for those who have not been to Hong Kong to still participate easily. We asked broad questions like, "What's your favorite Asian dish?" and "What Asian culinary festival have you attended, or would you like to attend?" And we gave the sponsor an opportunity to offer special "Pro Tips" about Hong

Kong, such as "Hong Kong has over 60 Michelin-starred restaurants" with a link to their website. This provided relevant insight to our chatters without becoming an hour of "buy my stuff" or "visit my destination" from our sponsor.

What's particularly gratifying is when we actually see tweeps in real time say "I'm adding Hong Kong to my travel list," or "I was already planning to go, and now I can't wait to try these suggestions." We actually have had chatters make plans to meet in person for a meal, travel together, or even plan a trip. We've been asked by our tweeps to consider hosting a FoodTravel-Chat tour, so perhaps that will come in the future as well.

Our #FoodTravelChat community consists of food travel enthusiasts from around the world. They are culinary and hospitality professionals, active travelers, bloggers and journalists, tourism board members, and people who aspire to travel more. The one thing they have in common is their love for food and travel combined.

Many of them are experienced travelers looking for ideas on where to go for the first time or where to find unique hotels, restaurants, products, and experiences when they do a deeper dive into a destination they already have visited. They tend to entertain at home, sharing food and travel stories with others. The chat is often an extension of what they already enjoy talking about in their offline lives.

A very important part of the chat is actually seeing images of the food and travel destinations in the questions or the answers. People just don't engage as much with plain text tweets because they want to see for themselves what you're talking about. For some questions, we actually ask for "Photos please!" when we think it will help.

We also started to write content for our website that can be shared during #FoodTravelChat. As our relationships grew with destinations and brands, we would also use #FoodTravelChat as an additional place to share articles we have posted to FoodTravelist.com.

For example, we received a hosted visit to the Caribbean island of Nevis a few years ago. We continue to use photos of the West Indian buffet and pig roast we had there when a question about "memorable unique dining experiences" pops up. Likewise, you may often see us respond to a question about "favorite outdoor activities" with a photo and description of horseback riding, river rafting, or wildlife-watching in Montana, even if we have not been there recently.

This approach provides additional opportunities for exposing people to the offerings of brands and destinations we enjoy, long after our own experience with them has occurred. The value of providing ongoing coverage through our Twitter chat means that brands, destinations, and experiences that work with us get extra opportunities. They appear in front of our audience beyond the original agreement we may have made for an article or social media coverage. "Pro Tips" we tweet during sponsored chats contain links to relevant content on FoodTravelist.com or to sponsor sites. This also helped drive traffic to our site and to the sites of those who support our efforts, enhancing our value and deepening our relationships.

As a result of this carefully curated and continual effort, the chat became a vibrant community. Chatters come back every week to share with us and their #FoodTravelChat friends. Many of our chatters have participated since its beginning.

We now have hundreds of people that join every week to talk about their food travels or discover new dishes and places. The sense of community is strong, and people don't want to miss out or be forgotten. People will tag us during the week, and we'll see questions asked during the chat hour that receive answers long after the chat has finished. Sometimes, there's an unofficial "after chat party" where chatters who want to continue chatting do so even though the official chat has concluded.

What's even more gratifying is that when some-one is not going to be able to participate, he or she will often tweet with the hashtag to inform the community that they're sorry they will miss it, but they'll "see" everyone next week. That is quite unusual and a testament to the strong sense of belonging this chat has created.

Working with Sponsors

Working with sponsors is an important aspect of our overall business plan. We've had the priv-ilege of working with large destinations with big budgets as well as small brands with very limited resources. Every sponsorship is a unique experience and requires relationship building, trust, and understanding.

Our business goal from the start for Food Trav-elist has been to build long-lasting destination and brand relationships. #FoodTravelChat has been an extension of that goal. We've had many sponsors who have remained with #FoodTravel-Chat over the years. Some destinations have participated in a program by which they spon-sor one chat per quarter for a year. And some brands sponsored a single chat and had such a great experience that they sponsored another a few months later and continue to sponsor chats periodically every year.

One of the challenges is pricing sponsorships

and, in turn, ensuring we get paid in a timely manner. As the chat has grown over the years, we've adjusted our pricing accordingly. We have a standard price sheet but most often create a custom package designed specifically for each sponsor.

When we started the chat, we charged a few hundred dollars for a chat sponsorship. We have since expanded our offerings with various levels ranging from that price for a basic sponsorship to over a thousand dollars for highly integrated sponsorships that include graphics, direct messages, pro tips, and links as well as other promotional efforts.

We also subscribe to Hashtracking, a paid social media tool that monitors hashtags. Through Hashtracking, we can closely watch our hashtag and create reports on the number of tweets, reach, and number of chatters very easily. When a topic performs especially well or there is an upcoming relevant event, we know we can create a new post or highlight an existing one to drive traffic back to the site.

We've discovered that there are a lot of "holidays" that serve as great chat topics and also lend themselves to roundup posts. For example, National Bakery Day is celebrated every year. This is an opportunity to center a chat around favorite bakeries across the world. Plus, we can write a new post or link to a previous one on the website about favorite bakeries we have visited. If we're able to find a bakery that is interested in sponsoring the chat, so much the better.

We often receive press releases from PR companies seeking coverage for brands or destinations tying their offerings to an associated holiday such as National Potato Month, International Pickles Week, or World Cocktail Day. Seasonal holidays or happenings also make for great crossovers between posts and chats. They take advantage of the things people are already talking about on Twitter and elsewhere such as "Harvest Feasts Around The World" or "Favorite Summer Road Trips."

Moving Forward

I have invested a lot of time and energy into developing #FoodTravelChat. Twitter is a platform that I don't own, so I can never be quite sure if it will remain useful and viable as a part of my business. But for now, I intend to keep #FoodTravelChat running as long as I can manage it. Although in some ways it has taken on a life of its own, I still enjoy producing it, connecting with my Twitter friends every week, and having another value for prospective partners that not everyone else can offer.

Every week, I meet new people who share my passion for food travel and have wonderful stories and photos to share. And I feel responsible for managing this community that I have helped create to ensure that it is there for those who rely on it for pleasure, information, entertainment, and communicating with one another.

We describe #FoodTravelChat as a "virtual global dinner party" that brings people together from around the world for one hour a week to talk about their favorite food travel experiences. We encourage them to explore the Food-Travelist.com website, and I believe that the community we have created brings us all a little bit closer together. That alone is worth the effort.

* * *

Sue Reddel is Co-Founder of Food Travelist, which connects food travelers around the world with relevant brands, destinations, and experiences. She specializes in reducing travel hassles and shares tips on how to get the most out of every visit. An expert with 30 years experience in integrated marketing communications she is also an adjunct professor at Roosevelt University and a nature lover.

NEXT STEPS...

If you made it through this entire book, you've devoured the top advisory highlights from professional travel writers with a huge amount of writing experience.

I hope you learned a few things, and feel empowered to take on this fantastic job.

If you enjoyed the book **please consider leaving a review on Amazon** and other book-selling and book review platforms. It will genuinely help more wannabe travel writers see the advice contained inside, as well as acting as a small appreciative nod to the more than 30 people who pooled their words to make this book possible.

PLUS:: BONUS EXTRA!
A free cheatsheet containing 125+ travel publications that accept freelance articles.
Go to TravelWriteEarn.com to view/download

PLUS:: BONUS EXTRA 2!
Consider joining the '100 Pitches' Facebook group, a small group of friendly, helpful freelance writers who inspire each other to pitch

well and as often as possible.
Search for '100 pitches' on Facebook to view/join

Thanks again, and good luck. The world, and an exciting new career, awaits.

James Durston

Travel Write Earn Facebook group: www.facebook.com/travelwriteearn

BONUS CHAPTERS:

Sample chapters from other books in the Travel Write Earn series follow below.

CHAPTER 3 FROM TRAVEL WRITE EARN BOOK 1

How To Sell Travel Stories - Advice From Editors

THE BEST PITCH I EVER RECEIVED

So what would a perfect pitch look like? Inevitably every editor around the world has his or her own preferences. Here I'll lay out how I request pitches come to me. I think most editors would agree that the format I'll describe makes it quick and easy to decide whether the story is right for their publication or not. That's really what a good pitch is all about.

It's staggering to me that in a decade of assigning content, I've only once received a pitch that landed in this format without my requesting it first. I have the author's permission to show you that pitch - the best I've ever received - which I've pasted at the end of this chapter.

In my idyllic editorial world, the perfect pitch would look like this:

Headline

50-word summary

More info (100 words)

Imagery

This succinctly lays out what the story is about and allows me to quickly judge whether it's something I (and my readers) might be interested in. But beyond this the perfect pitch would have one quality - I wouldn't need to change a thing or ask any questions. And, hopefully, when the piece arrived, I wouldn't make a single edit or source a single image, and could immediately load the thing into the content management system and hit publish. That's what editors dream of and what writers should aspire to.

Reality is never so glitch-free and even when I get pitches in line with the above, it's rare I'll assign immediately without at least a little discussion about the main theme or angle of the piece, ask some questions about fact sourcing, possible interviews and so on. But the recipe above is a good clean start, and here's why.

Headline

Journalism courses pre-Internet always taught that the headline should be the last thing you write, once you've written the story and actually know what it's about. Many writers that file to me don't bother with even a cursory attempt at a headline, probably assuming that the sub-editors or I have that covered.

That's the first mistake you can make in a pitch to an online publication. Firstly, it's rare these days that an online publication, unless it's huge, will have a team of sub-editors. The journalism profession has undergone a bundling of roles, where the writer is the editor and often the photographer or at least the photo-researcher too, as well as the Facebooker, Tweeter, search-engine-optimizer and coffee-getter. The headline is, for an Internet story, also a pitch to the reader: read this! You cannot not click this story! Miss this and you miss out! It only takes a few seconds' thought to see why the Internet requires us to flip the old school headline lesson on its head.

Flicking through a magazine or newspaper, your reader is held captive, eyes scanning maybe three or four headlines in the news section, down to one headline over up to eight pages in the features well. Competition between stories here is tiny to non-existent. There is context everywhere - pictures, captions and other snippets of text will all provide information to the reader about the article in attractive formats. And for that reason, you'll sometimes see feature headlines in a hardcopy magazine that tell you nothing about the story you might be about to read. Forefront is style, or a clever pun (I hate puns), or some graphic flourish. So "Truly, Madly, Deeply" (I also hate film title headlines) becomes a headline for a story about a love affair between two psychiatrists. "The Dark Knight" becomes a headline for a winemaker who makes wine in the depths of a cave.

If online writers construct headlines like this, their stories die, quickly. Scan a content-heavy website and you may have up to a hundred stories crammed together, bumping and overlapping and jostling for the reader's attention. There are few or no contextual add-ons. The stories that get the traffic are promoted and propped up so they can get even more traffic, the stories that no one reads are quickly removed from the front pages, relegated to the bottomless abyss of "the archive." CNN in the United States has hourly traffic targets and anything that isn't pulling its weight is swiftly replaced. This survival of the fittest style of programming a site doesn't depend entirely on the headline, but it plays a key role in making readers decide to click or not.

It's said that 80% of people read headlines and just 20% read the story. So how do we convert browsers into readers? What makes for a good headline online? There's no single formula you should follow each time you write a head. Different stories will require different treatments and good headline writing is as much a craft as good writing is, even in the Internet age. But say my editor said to me one morning, "We're going to be 100,000 clicks short of our target this month - I need you to get a story up that'll cover that shortfall over the next 24 hours." In this case, which is perfectly possible in online publishing, my go-to formula for a headline that I know will generate above average clicks would look something like this:

Number + superlative + thing + place = clicks

Yes, that's a list. Scream all you want about lists being the editorial equivalent of a deep-fried pizza - I'm here to tell you what works in the minds of traffic-needy editors, and lists work. For psychological reasons that have been explored and interpreted in multifarious articles, Internet users love to click a list. And given that most, if not all online editors have traffic targets, lists are an easy option to keep traffic high. Here are the headlines for some of my high-traffic assigns while at CNN:

World's 50 most delicious foods

20 of the world's most iconic skyscrapers

World's 100 best beaches

27 sights that will remind you how incredible Earth is

Asia's 10 greatest street food cities

10 things Italy does better than anywhere else

World's happiest countries: 1 to 187

15 unusual places to spend a night

19 greatest bonus-busting experiences

10 most beautiful university buildings

I've selected these because they fit the formula I describe above and because they were commissions I personally made. They're not the top ten stories from CNN Travel during my tenure there. But a glance at the top stories over a period shows that the general rule above holds for most of the top stories by pageview. Below is a snapshot of the top 20 stories published by CNNGo up to November 2012 (when CNNGo was disbanded and merged into the wider CNN website as CNN Travel):

	Page
1.	Home
2.	World's 50 most delicious foods
3.	The world's coolest nationalities: Where do you rank?
4.	http://www.cnngo.com
5.	Shanghai city
6.	Asia's most sinful cities
7.	20 of the world's most iconic skyscrapers
8.	Hong Kong city
9.	World's 50 best beaches
10.	America's most sinful cities
11.	Tokyo city
12.	10 of the world's most hated airports
13.	Bangkok city
14.	7 sexy skinny dips
15.	Singapore city
16.	World's 50 most delicious drinks
17.	World's 12 worst tourist traps
18.	Seoul city
19.	40 Taiwanese foods we can't live without
20.	World's sexiest accents

Excepting the home and city landing pages (1, 4, 5, 8, 11, 13, 15, 18), every one of these follows the rule to some extent. Numbers (50, 20, 10...), superlatives (most delicious, coolest, most sinful, most iconic, best...), things (foods, cities, skyscrapers, beaches...) and places (world, America, Asia, Taiwan...). At the time of recording (November 2012) the top 14 stories here all had pageviews in excess of 1 million. They will all have a lot more too by now (November 2016).

"But wait," I hear you think. "This book is meant for travel writers - are these strictly travel stories? Are lists of sinful cities and sexy accents now game for travel pitches?"

This is slightly off topic for this chapter, but let me give a quick answer just to quench your curiosity: those pieces fit for CNNGo. Which is why good writers research the publication they want to pitch, before pitching. I will concede my supervising editor and I struggled a little with the "America's sinful cities" idea, especially considering the furor that erupted when we published Asia's most sinful cities. See Chapter 14 for an entertaining tale about that piece. What swayed us was the knowledge that a) we had a great writer doing the American version whom we knew would write it brilliantly, research it thoroughly and be highly entertaining, and b) it would get huge traffic.

That's not to say all stories likely to get a million hits are a guaranteed commission, nor is it to say high-traffic lists are the only stories worth considering. But in a 50-50 situation they may help your idea fall on the positive side of that line.

Take another look at that snapshot of the top stories above and you may notice a dilemma for you as a travel writer. These are clearly not the kinds of stories you write having just gone somewhere or done something. Most lists like these are exercises in creative research, "desk writes" as I call them, that can be done with a Google connection and a couple of spare evenings. Sure you could at least part-fund your three-night beach excursion with a few pieces like this, but that's hardly the same as traveling to Bali as a travel writer to write about Bali is it? Chapter 9 goes into this in more depth, but it's worth asking yourself what kind of writer you are, or want to be, or are happy to be. That can define, or at least guide, your story ideas and your pitches.

Other kinds of headline

No one wants to write or read lists all day, every day. Some don't want to write lists at all, any day. I, as a list-hungry editor, think those who avoid or refuse to consider lists among their oeuvre are needlessly skipping by piles of easy cash, albeit small piles. Younger writers don't seem to have this problem. Lists are a major part of the media they consume, and so it's natural they'll fit into the landscape of their work. It seems to be older writers who feel that lists in some way are a corruption of their craft. And I do hear you. A website full of nothing but lists is like a banquet table covered in nothing but desserts. Tasty, for a while, but hardly nutritious. Which is why traditional feature stories remain important to many travel websites.

So what's the formula to a non-list headline? There isn't one and I won't try to reduce this entire art to something mathematical. But I will still argue that in order to sell your story, you need to be thinking about the headline from the outset. So if your story's about the fishermen of Inle Lake in Myanmar, what's going to really sell the piece to your editor? Don't forget, in turn, he or she will be thinking about how to sell this piece to their managers and eventually readers.

What's unique or special or enthralling or gripping about your story? What's the miss-it-miss-out quality? Here are some categories of headline that can at least frame your story idea. Each example headline is a real story that I assigned (and in most cases probably wrote the headline for too) or is a real story I saw on the Internet and liked.

The thing that it is

Some stories are their own headlines. To try to embellish these is not only unnecessary, it may even detract from the essence and intrigue of the piece.

Gallery: Myanmar's leg rowers of Inle Lake

Vietnam's farmer violinists

The sulfur slaves of Kawah Ijen

Riding shotgun in the Gumball 3000

The people who create their own "countries"

First person

Travel writing in its purest form is a description of an experience with the thoughts and personal interpretations that come to the writer during a trip. First-person headlines underline this connection between the writer, the experience and the reader.

Why I climb insanely tall buildings with my bare hands

Why I hope to die at 75

How I got over my fear of flying

The drink that nearly knocked me out with one sniff

SEO

Search engine optimization - modifying content to match what people search for - is the steamed cauliflower on our editorial plates. We know it's good for us, but it's just so yucky. Entire books and thousands, possibly millions of blog and web posts have been written about editorial attempts to second-guess Google. I'm not going to even touch it here, except to say that SEO-derived headlines, and indeed story ideas, can and do work. I even once assigned a story based on the top Google searches for travel: "Time travel with your cat: How Google sees your vacation plans."

Best French restaurants in Paris

Where is Okinawa?

Where to get married: World's best wedding venues

How tos

This kind of headline requires a certain type of article and in many cases they're a subset of the SEO category. If the idea is good, these headlines can be highly clickable.

How to take better travel photos

How to fly first-class for free

How to be a Hong Kong local: 10 tips for faking it (ok a how to-list combo)

How to become a Bollywood extra

Teasers

The teaser headline can often be considered click-baity and annoying. But if you're not gratuitous about it, they can work.

The world's best airport is …

Possibly the year's greatest travel photo

World's happiest country is where?

Questions

Old-school journos will say, "You're not writing articles to ask questions, you're writing articles to answer them." But nothing gets to the heart of an angle like the question you probably asked when the idea came to you.

What's it like to be crucified?

Is massage good for you or does it just feel nice?

Is this the inventor of bubble tea?

What's life like in paradise?

Do you care if your hotel has good art?

As I write these I realize this list of headline

categories could go on for a few pages. Which underlines the point that there is no formula. The trick, the craft, the art and the science of a good headline has to come from your idea of what the most important or interesting aspect of the story is. And how can you boil that down to eight or ten words, in the style of your chosen publication?

I consider the headline the absolute key component of your pitch. If I like it, I'll certainly read on. A good headline that sums up the story and also fits the voice and style of my publication gives me confidence that you know what you're doing, that you're a proper pro who understands the nature of this business and working with you may not just be good for the site and for our readers (and by extension myself) but could be the start of an ongoing relationship that makes my job a lot easier and more enjoyable.

Now comes the disclaimer: unless you're writing a list and follow the headline formula described above, your headline probably won't make it onto the published page. Editors, simply through years of experience, will have a much better feel for what their publication needs and each editor will have their own personal preferences to boot. But that's not your concern. You're concerned with selling a story. What happens after that is out of your hands. Your headline is designed to sell your story to your editor.

And that's as far as you should plan.

A good headline is an introduction. You need to back it up with meaningful information about the story itself. If the headline is a doorway, you also need to describe the room - at least the basic furnishings. You can think of your pitch as a micro-version of a feature. The best online content has a great, clickable headline, and then backs it up with superb content. The headline pulls you in, the story gets it shared. And the instant you back up your possibly clickbait headline with good content, it ceases to be clickbait and becomes a great article. A successful story fulfills the promise of its headline. And the best pitches back up their working headlines with great summaries.

So now to the best pitch I ever received, from a freelance travel writer named Richard Mellor. This was not right for my publication at the time, so I declined the story, but I know he did soon sell it to the Independent On Sunday and also Passport, Monarch Airline's in-flight magazine.

After connecting with me on LinkedIn, here's what he wrote:

Hi James,

Thanks for connecting with me, much appreciated. Reading about LE PAN made me realize my forthcoming trip, next week, is very relevant. I'm not sure if you're the person to whom I should pitch, but here goes anyway:

GRUB WITH THE GRAPES — BORDEAUX'S FOOD REVOLUTION

Sell: Gordon Ramsay's arrival clinches it: the old wine city has become a new food city

With his just-opened Pressoir-d'Argent, Gordon Ramsay joins Joel Robuchon and Philippe Etchebest, host of the French version of Kitchen Nightmares, in recently opening in Bordeaux. Throw in Miles, co-winner of Gallic bible Le Fooding's recent Restaurant of the Year award, and the old wine city has suddenly become a new food city.

Other reasons to visit are much-improved museums, a once-crummy riverside made pretty again and, of course, those grand cru vineyards. There's also a 'go now' imperative, before lads and luddites arrive: Bordeaux is a host-city for summer's Euro 2016 international football tournament, while 2017 will see the completion of a high-speed TGV line from Paris.

I've been invited on a press trip to visit Bordeaux and Pressoir-d'Argent next week.

Hope this might work. Please feel free to email me on ric***or@gmail.com (I can explain...!) if it does.

All my best,

Richard

Great headline, great sell, good extra details, good research into my publication, succinct and timely. There's no way to improve this.

* * *

Order this book on Amazon:

How To Sell Travel Stories - Advice From Editors

CHAPTER 1
FROM TRAVEL
WRITE EARN
BOOK 2

Why Editors Don't Reply: And other insights about freelance travel writing

A few months ago I wrote to dozens of freelance travel writers and professional bloggers to ask: what's your biggest challenge? What's the most frustrating problem you have as a freelancer?

I've been an editor for the last decade or so, and though I've spent a few years freelancing, these years have been scattered, so I went to source to discover the problems full-time freelancers face on a daily basis.

More than 50 wrote back to me with their problems. Some were so frustrated with the trade they had given up. "I never pitch to magazines or papers any more," wrote one. "All I can tell you is that trying to sell a travel story these days is like pulling teeth, unless you know the editor personally."

But others obliged. The queries generally broke down into common areas such as pitching, money, contacting editors and more, so I've used these to chapterize the book. A few more didn't fit these themes and so appear at the end in the miscellaneous section.

I hope these 40 questions (and their answers) will be useful to those just starting out on the adventure of breaking into travel writing, and also those who have been at it a while and, perhaps like the writer I quote above, need someone else's angle on some of the more frequent challenges faced.

So here are my personal tidbits of advice for the best ways to resolve or at least ease the pain of indie travel writing as a livelihood.

PS: I'm always happy to hear from and engage with readers and freelancers about the things I write about, and especially things I haven't written about. Feel free to look up more details on writing and pitching for a travel market or to contact me on my blog - www.travelwriteearn.com.

THE COMMONEST COMPLAINT

1. Editor (non)communication
AKA: "Why are editors such cold, silent, uncommunicative BASTARDS?"

By far the most common grievance was this. Conveyed with varying degrees of murderous animosity, this top lament, dripping with exasperation, is one I think all freelancers who pitch will have experienced. Some sample quotes:

> "Pitching articles day after day while receiving little or no response is such a waste of time when you make your living as writer."

> "If the email is never opened, it doesn't matter how good and targeted it is. I'm seriously thinking about going back to mailing paper queries."

> "After five sends of the query to two different e-mails ... I still have no reply ... I find this not only rude but outrageous ... and I have checked them off my query list. I simply can't waste my time and creative juices on that kind of treatment."

> "I don't need lengthy explanations as to why my pitch didn't work, but ra-

ther quick, helpful guidance helping me place ideas that are a good fit. An editor recently got back to me saying in one sentence 'I have too many food stories and features on China and Thailand, and short on pitches on Japan, Burma and Malaysia.' This was super helpful."

"I don't really buy it when editors say 'do you know how busy we are?' My answer is yes I do, because I worked on a travel desk for 12 years. We're all busy. My favourite UK editor (who shall remain nameless) always gets back within 2 days (usually same day) with just the word 'no' or 'yes'. It's all I need to know!"

Editors are not too busy

Being ignored is never pleasant is it. And just to prove that I really do understand all those who mentioned this problem, I make a conscious effort to reply to all pitches I receive, even if it's a cursory "No, but thanks."

Let me start by agreeing with the last quotee. Many of these complaints came with some variation of the qualifier: "I know editors are crazily, insanely busy...". This is a myth that needs to be busted.

Editors are not the busiest people outside of Donald Trump's Twitter crisis team, no matter how much they'd like you to believe it. I'm probably the first editor to even contemplate busting this myth, because of the excuses it allows us to make. Sorry, I can't answer that email, I can't take that call, I can't make lunch or dinner this week or next week or next month or next year, no mom I can't come to aunt Sylvie's funeral, sorry hun I can't make the birth of our son, I can't talk, I can't breathe, I can't even work I'm so damn busy.

Enough. Yes editors are busy. But the busiest editors are those who have no freelance budget and have to write everything they publish. We're not interested in them. Commissioning editors, or editors lucky enough to work on a title that uses freelancers, are certainly not too busy to read your email (I guarantee they did. At least a few lines. No one wants to miss out on a great story, even if it means reading 100 bad ideas first). They're not too busy to send a brief cursory reply (they just don't want to). And they're certainly not busier than the full-time freelancer trying to feed a family and pay bills and write stories and source pictures and find the next assignment. These editors start work at 9, finish at 6 and get a guaranteed, can't-complain wage slip at the end of every month, no matter how many articles they write or edit. They get all the usual employee benefits, zero risk and could eat out for free at a nice hotel or restaurant three days a week or more should they want.

We don't need to pander to the egos of this blessed crowd, despite our co-dependence.

At the same time, we shouldn't expect them to reply to every pitch.

It may be polite, you may think it would make their lives easier in the long run by guiding you to pitch ideas better aligned to their needs, you might consider it a painless way to extend the simplest of professional courtesies, but actually that's not your call. They're doing their job the way they think works best for them, so you need to do yours they way that's best for you.

That means retaining your professionalism in the face of such abhorrent insolence(!)

So, why might an editor not want to reply to your pitch?

Nine out of 10 editors prefer some other story

The first thing to realise is that no reply really does mean no thanks, at least 95% of the time. As I said, your email did get read, so if the story was of interest you would have had a reply probably within a few days. So straight away we're looking at 19 out of 20 'no responses' meaning no interest.

Why no reply? Editors are human, and humans tend toward self-interest and self-preservation.

Self-interest

"This email is of no use to me," goes the thinking. "Delete." The therapeutic effects of deleting emails and at least trying to reach inbox zero, however doomed the attempt, outweigh the small niggling voice in the head saying "It would be polite to reply. They'd appreciate it."

Note that at that moment the editor is looking at and concerned with "an email." Not a person, not a struggling freelancer waiting like a forgotten puppy at the other end of the Interweb. A cold, lifeless, useless email.

And he or she knows that another email, possibly a useful one with an idea they like, will be along very soon. There's no need to spend any time or effort on this one.

Self-preservation

Second, sometimes an editor, possibly after having had a bottle of fine wine and a Death By Chocolate dessert at lunch, will reply to a failed pitch. And it's like making eye contact with the beggar. (Apologies for the obtuse comparison. Beggars deserve better!) This happened to me often. You don't want to be like the heartless masses who walk by without so much as a glance. So you acknowledge them. Maybe you even smile. And suddenly they latch on, their eye won't let you go, they're looking at you and suddenly they're talking to you and you just want to walk to the store to get a pack of chips and a bottle of gin, and you wonder why oh why did I make eye contact, I knew this would happen, it pains me it really does, but no, you cannot have my money, I just wanted to buy some dinner, god why did I do it, I have to stop making eye contact with beggars. Until the next extravagant lunch, of course.

That initial email can lead to more emails, and if you're really caught up in the moment of an editor finally engaging with you, maybe even a phone call. And there are few things editors dread more than phone calls from writers whose pitch they just rejected.

Those are just two reasons editors don't reply to failed pitches - explanations, even if they're not watertight excuses.

The follow-up

The 1 in 20 non-replies that still could lead to a job could occur for various reasons: out of office, spam folder, busy putting together a complicated feature for publishing in the next couple of days, simply can't be bothered looking at/responding to pitches today, and a dozen more.

How do you tell if your non-reply is in the 95% or the 5%? And what do you do if it's in the 5%?

Well, this is the crux of the question. There's a reason this was the most mentioned complaint from the writers I polled: unfortunately there's no simple answer.

The only way to get information out of your target editors is to follow up. And despite what I said above phone calls are most effective. I'd suggest (and as an editor have no problem with) a follow-up email the day or possibly two days after the original pitch and a phone call a couple days after that follow-up email (if no reply to that either).

Yes, I said "the day after." Many writers I've listened to ponder anxiously about waiting a week, or two weeks, or 18 days to follow up as if they're lovestruck teenagers squirming over their courting strategy. Wrong. You're a professional writer, he or she is a professional editor, and you just need to know what's what. It's best to do that while your email is still fresh and they don't have to go scrolling too far down their inbox (or trash folder) to find it.

Disclaimer: this works if you're dealing with an editor who has autonomy and can assign or reject ideas solo and as they come in (which is most). Some platforms however commission by committee, with weekly or monthly meetings to decide what gets assigned. Others state in their writer's guidelines that it can take up to six or eight weeks for them to make a decision. Details inside writer guidelines can often be taken with a spoonful of salt though, and as long as you abide by any direct feedback you get after following up, I see no problem in harassing them at least once.

Be direct and concise

Importantly, you don't want to become known as "that annoying freelancer who won't leave me alone." So in both email and phone call, be concise and direct. Small talk is for amateurs. You're intelligent enough to write your own scripts, but the message should be: I just want to make sure you read my pitch and understand why I think it's a great fit for you and your platform.

To save their time, have the exact subject line you used ready so they can search for your email easily, should they want. For this reason it helps to use a unique subject line in your query email, not a generic "Freelancer pitch" that could easily get lost among dozens. And if they've lost your email or prefer to hear you pitch over the phone, have your pitch in front of you and read it out as you've written it (and according to my advice!): potential headline/angle, quick summary, then, if they want more, further details (many more details about how exactly to pitch in my other book *How To Sell Travel Articles: Advice From Editors*: https://www.amazon.com/dp/B01N6H767B)

If you're the sensitive empathic type and can't bear the thought of firing off a follow-up email without some kind of excuse (you have a schedule to arrange, a travel itinerary to produce, a workload to organize, you're going to be out of Internet range for the next week, the spam folder has taken a dislike to your address recently) I'd strongly advise you to get over this little quirk. You're a pro who deals in information and you need to be businesslike, as well as pleasant and amiable, in these dealings. You'll come across far better and what matters is getting the information you need.

It's not personal

If you hear nothing on email and the editor refuses to take your call, you can reasonably assume you've been rejected. No hard feelings, take it on the chin, button yourself up and pitch elsewhere. You did your best. Remember: this doesn't mean they don't like you, it just means they didn't like this idea. What won't help your cause is getting emotional or offended. Striking non-replying titles off your query list as one quotee claims to have done above may feel gratifying in the short-term, but almost certainly deprives yourself more than it does the editor or title.

* * *

Order this book on Amazon:

Why Editors Don't Reply: And other insights about freelance travel writing

TRAVEL WRITE EARN

Insider insights into the world of travel writing, editing and publishing.

How To Sell Travel Stories: Advice From Editors

- How to write pitches/queries editors love to read
- Why headlines are the key ingredient when pitching to online platforms
- Which travel magazines and websites want your work, and how much they pay
- The best and worst pitches ever received
- How to 'brand' yourself as a writer worth hiring

All this and much more in this insightful, penetrating, straight-to-the-point book from a working editor who reveals why he buys certain pitches and bins others.

Why Editors Don't Reply: And Other

Insights About Freelance Travel Writing

Answering 40 real questions from working travel writers around the world, the second Travel Write Earn book (from www.travel-writeearn.com) focuses purely on the daily practicalities of being a working travel freelancer in the 21st century.

Why do so many editors ignore your pitches?
What time of day or of the week should you send a query to maximize your chances of success?
How can you convince an editor to buy a story he or she says they really don't need?
What can you do to maximize your fees and ensure prompt payment?
Should you offer to include pictures with your story?
Should you send a fully written piece or just an idea when pitching?
Can you pitch multiple editors at once?
What's the easiest and quickest way to find the exact editor to pitch and their email address?

All these and many more REAL QUESTIONS from real freelancers are answered by a working travel editor.

Made in United States
North Haven, CT
15 April 2022

18309417R00200